HOW TO DRAW HORSES

EVERYTHING YOU EVER WANTED TO KNOW ABOUT DRAWING
HORSES • HARDWARE • HISTORY • MYTHOLOGY

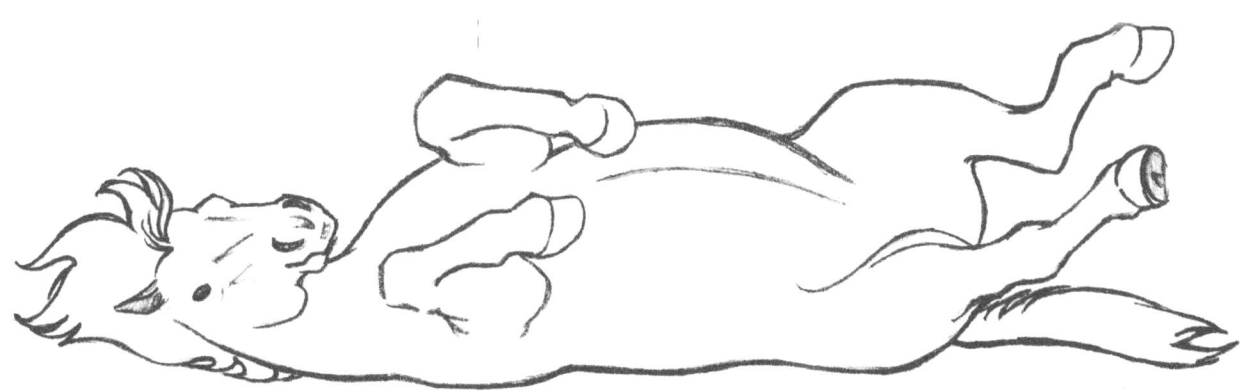

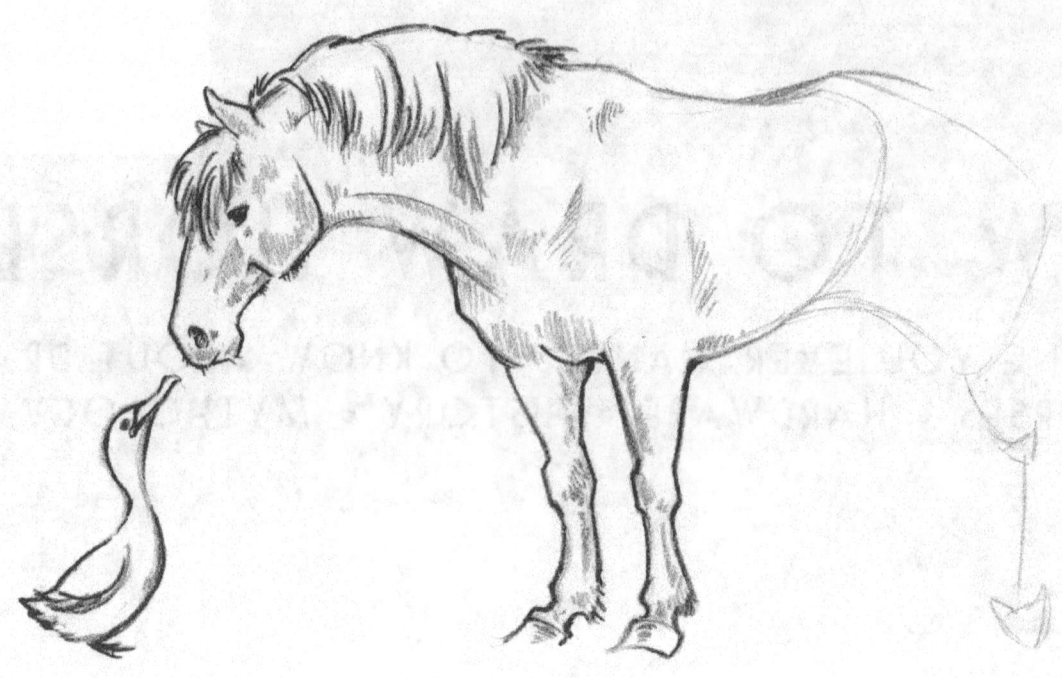

Dedicated to all the fierce individuals who keep the world safe for artists
and horse lovers everywhere.

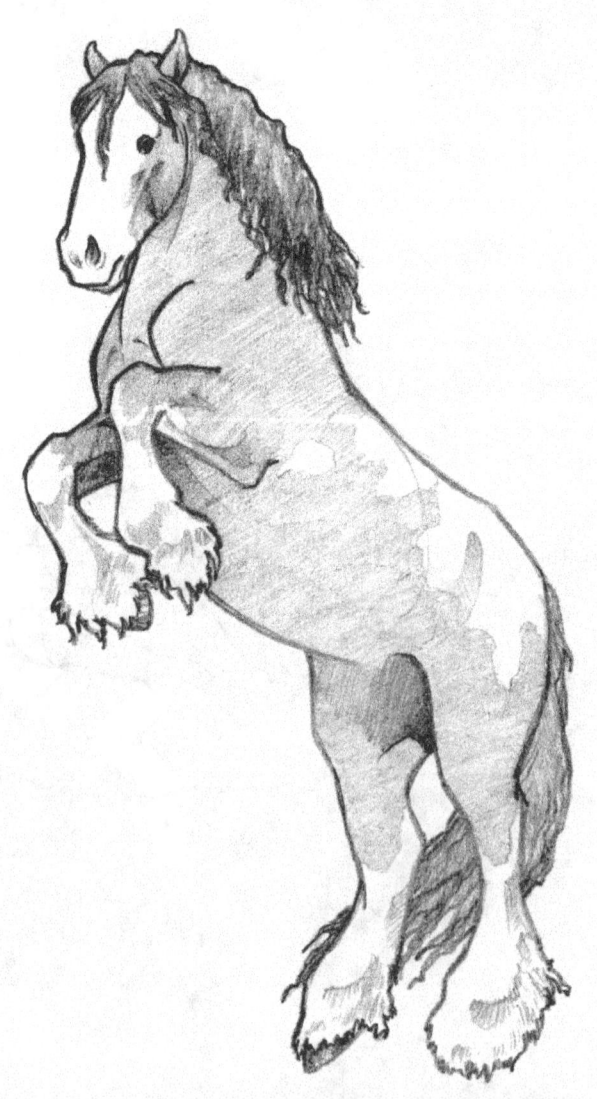

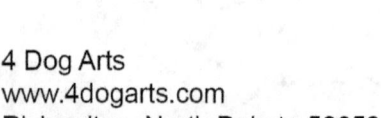
4 Dog Arts
www.4dogarts.com
Richardton, North Dakota 58652

ISBN-13: 978-1466460270
ISBN-10: 146646027X

INTRODUCTION

Welcome fellow arty-horse enthusiasts. Grab your art supplies and hunker down, because we are about to start some masterpieces! Don't have a huge, expensive studio and lots of spiffy art supplies? Perfect!

Mechanical pencil, available at any office supply store..

Kneaded eraser, usually looks like a gray turd.

Item 1.) Have some blasted realistic expectations. Nobody is an instant success. Artists draw tens to hundreds of thousands of images, and even the pros don't draw it perfect every time, so cut yourself some slack and have some fun.

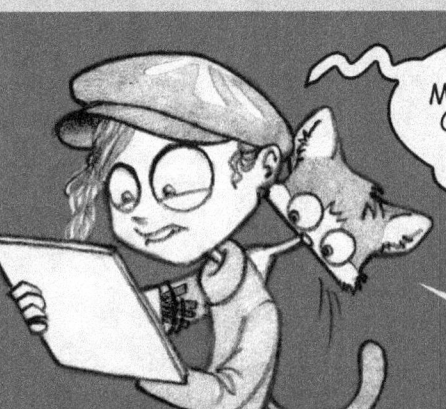

Shabby replacement for human interaction.

Item 2.) A little secret about getting that perfect, finished piece, with everything exactly where you want it without any blemishes or erase markings... nobody has it. When you have a sketch that you believe shows promise, get yourself some tracing paper. Trace your outlines, and trace your outlines again on the back. *THEN*, get your canvas/paper/whatever and using a hard pencil, trace your outlines to transfer for further use. Or skip the tracing paper and use a window or a light table. That's how it's done.

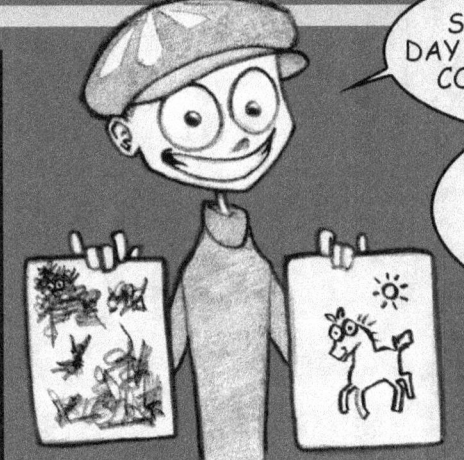

Sloppy sketches that do not deserve to live and 2 coffee stains.

Outlines that look like we had everything nice all along.

FOR MORE LIES AND MISINFORMATION, PLEASE CONTINUE...

Item 3.) Since we live in a digital world, it seems rational to make a note about painting software. The wizardry of all the available options will make your artist palate drool, but at the end of the day, it's no different than your pencil or ruler. It's still just a tool. So if you think that I would suggest than you rush out and buy something you actually didn't need, then you are mistaken. I am not prone to shady endorsements, falsely contributing to beliefs that with a few clicks, you could make up for years of training and practice. Not for free, anyway.

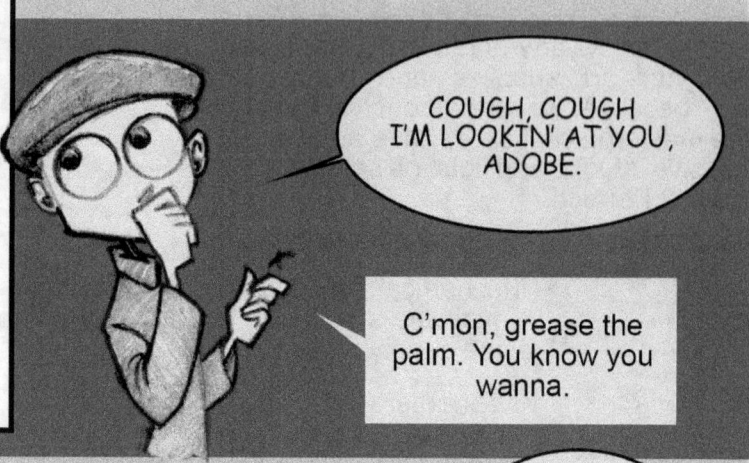

COUGH, COUGH I'M LOOKIN' AT YOU, ADOBE.

C'mon, grease the palm. You know you wanna.

Item 3.5) I actually love working digital, and I trust, you will too. The freeware out there such as Sumo Paint, Deviant Art Muro, or '*insert the latest big thing here*', are pretty sweet. As resources go, you can share with the art community at large, and receive thoughtful criticism for improvement such as, "LOL" and, "USUCK". Chances are, you already know all about this, because you have been surfing since you were in the womb.

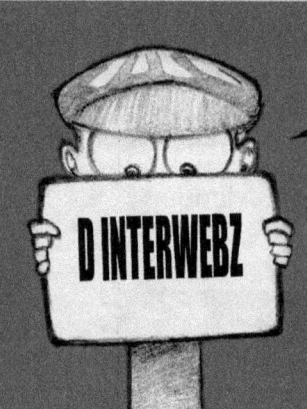

D INTERWEBZ

- SNIFF - HMMMM.... THE INTERNET SMELLS NUTTY.

Well, that about covers it. Might as well press on and follow the art-hack who's sense of fashion peaked while watching The Boondock Saints.

FEED ME FOOD MONKEY!

I AM GOING TO IGNORE THAT LAST COMMENT, UNTIL I CAN RESPOND WITH VARIOUS SOPHIS- TICATED AND REFINED EXPRESSIVE ADJECTIVES THAT MIGHT OTHERWISE LOOK, TO THE UNIN- FORMED OBSERVER, LIKE BAD WORDS.

GETTING STARTED

Before we begin, we're going to get familiar with a few basic shapes. These are the same, lame numbers you were probably asked to draw in school without really ever being told why.

So to start with, we're going to try to *unlearn* a few things...

Back is too short.

Legs are too long and spindly. Are we trying to draw a deer or a horse?

Rear Leg looks like it was put on by a retard tadpole.

Until now! Those boring little buggers are actually the fundamental building blocks for drawing.

(That means you can use 'em to make horses, bats, and stuff.)

And I could go on, but the point is, shapes are your friends, and they will save you wasted time and frustration on silly errors like the ones up above.

You get the idea...

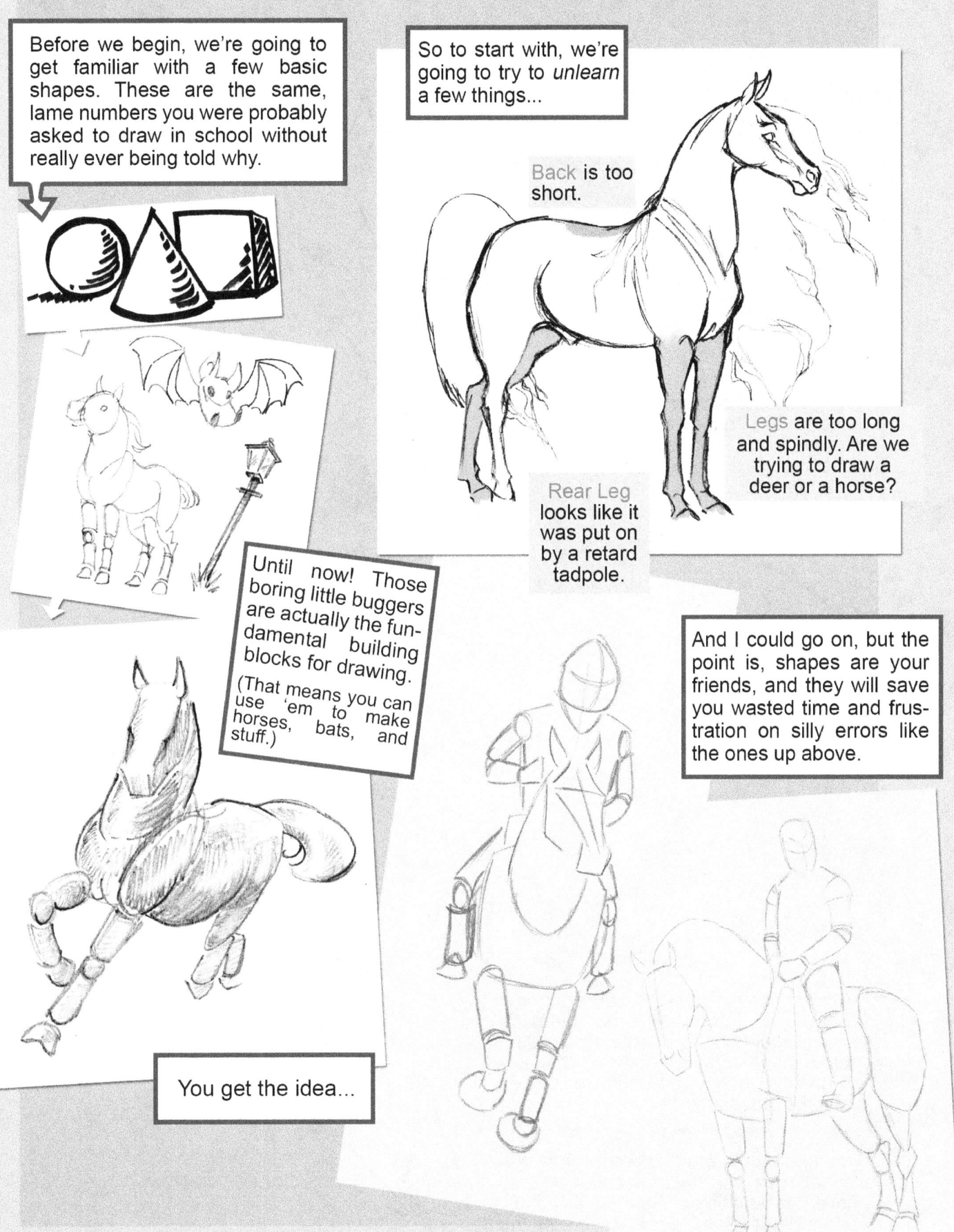

AWESOME ANATOMY

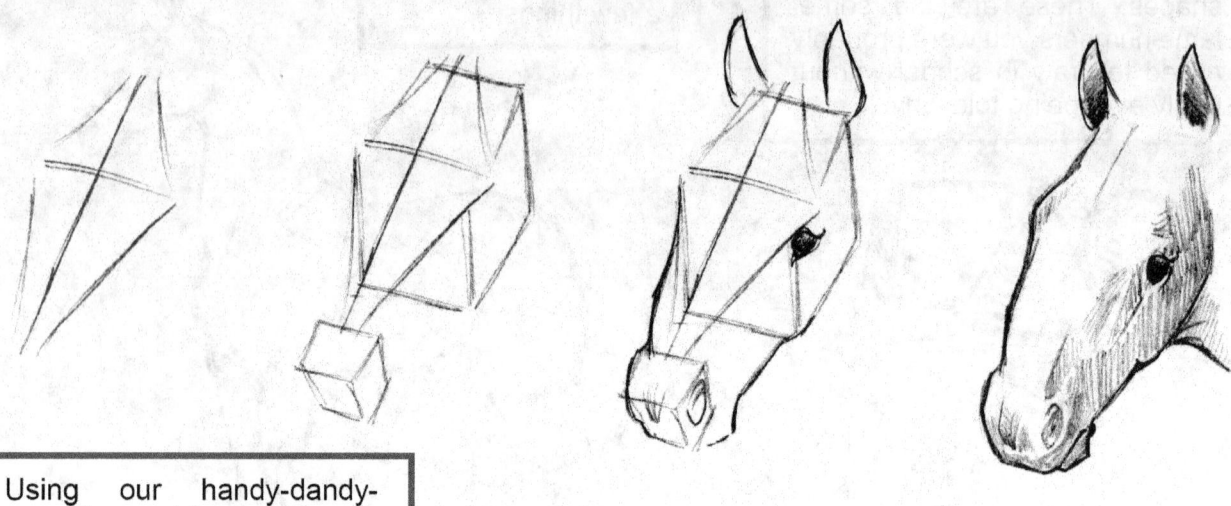

Using our handy-dandy-save-the-world shapes, we can construct any breed from any angle.

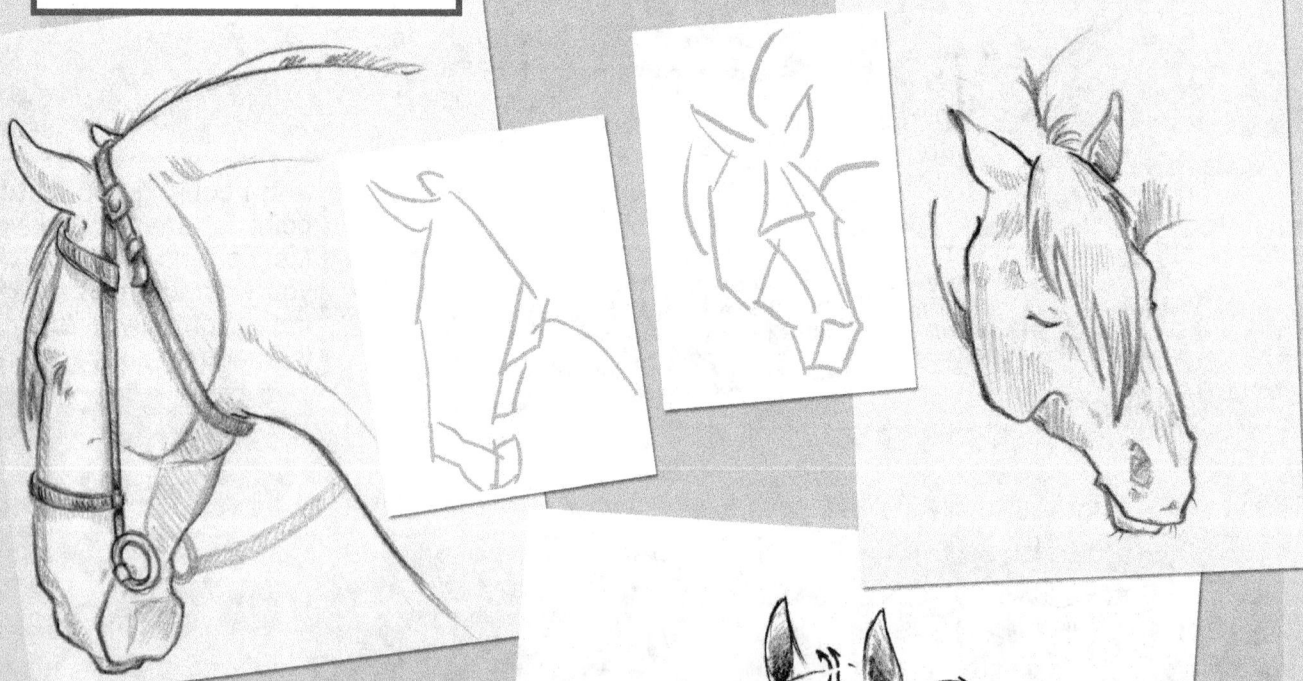

QUICK TIP: Horse hair is durable stuff. Unless your horse is in a mythical setting with a mane and tail that defies the laws of gravity, your lines should flow away from the hairline.

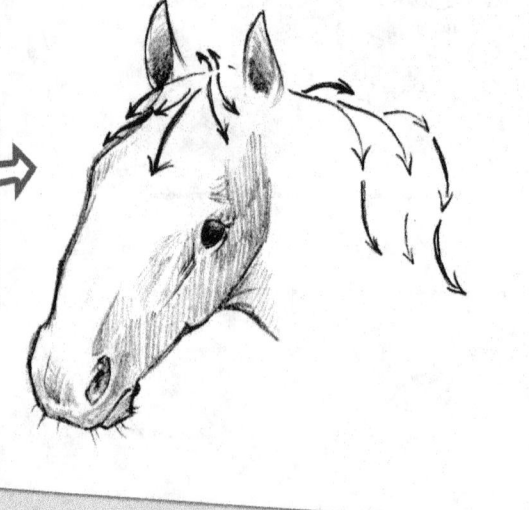

You don't really need to draw each, individual, SINGLE hair. (If you do, they have medication for that.) Tufts, lines, and well placed highlights will create the look you're going for.

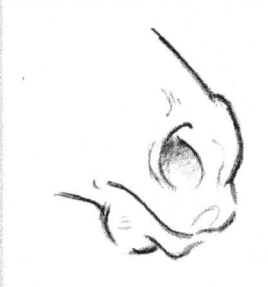

Think of the nose as a flopped number 6.

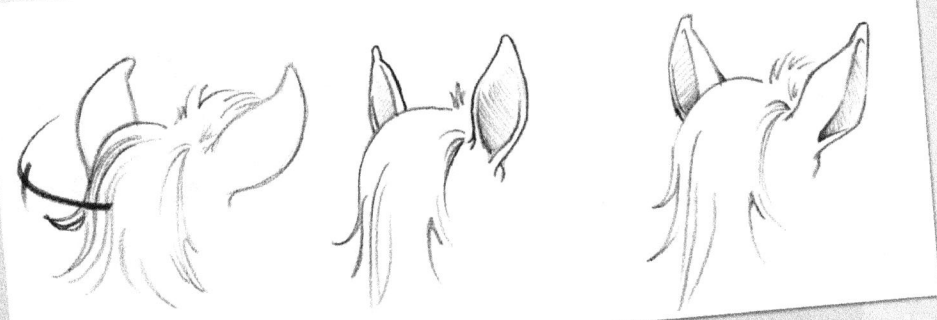

Ears can move together or independently in the direction of bears or treats. Ears also do a lot to express a horse's mood.

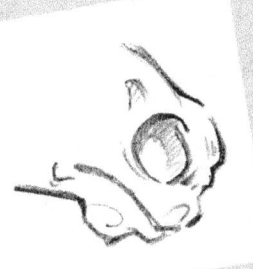

When excited, it flares to an O.

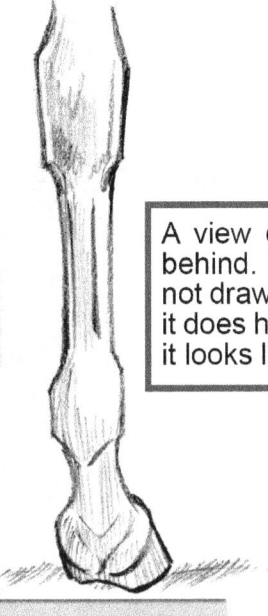

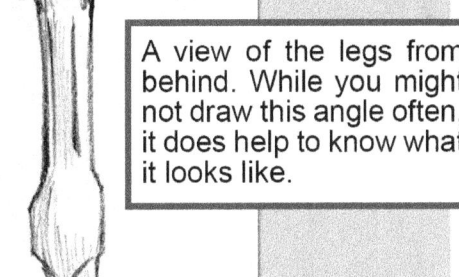

Looks like someone I know. Ha!

A view of the legs from behind. While you might not draw this angle often, it does help to know what it looks like.

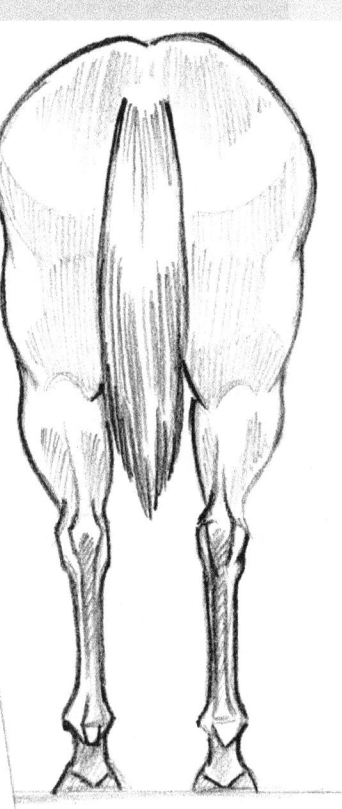

Being curious or reaching to treats will change it to an oval.

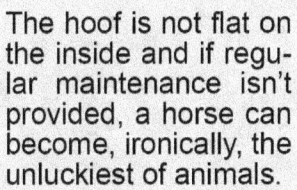

The hoof is not flat on the inside and if regular maintenance isn't provided, a horse can become, ironically, the unluckiest of animals.

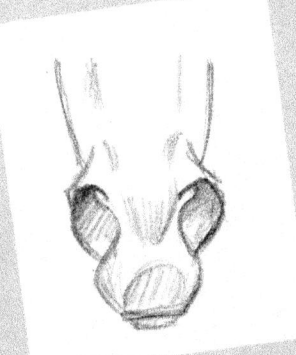

And here it is from the front.

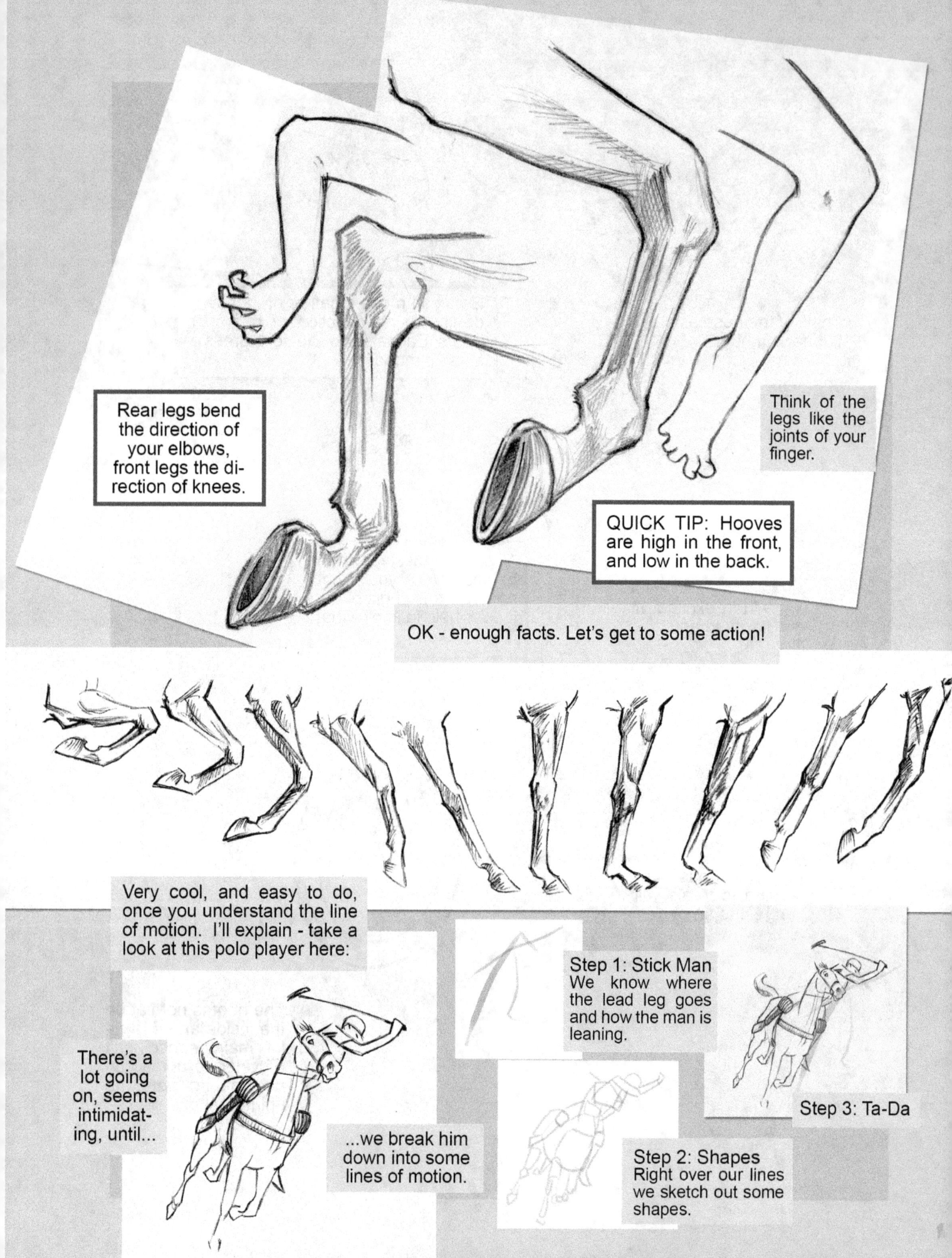

Rear legs bend the direction of your elbows, front legs the direction of knees.

Think of the legs like the joints of your finger.

QUICK TIP: Hooves are high in the front, and low in the back.

OK - enough facts. Let's get to some action!

Very cool, and easy to do, once you understand the line of motion. I'll explain - take a look at this polo player here:

There's a lot going on, seems intimidating, until...

...we break him down into some lines of motion.

Step 1: Stick Man We know where the lead leg goes and how the man is leaning.

Step 2: Shapes Right over our lines we sketch out some shapes.

Step 3: Ta-Da

THAT'S A NEGATORY GHOST RIDER

Asking my students to add a rider to their horse usually causes them to look at me in that certain type of way that I know they're pondering just exactly how deep the dark closets go in the mansion of my mind. But without humans, an artist is pretty limited. Also, it's freaking easy to add a rider to a horse's back.

Take this guy for example. He's off to a good start, and we don't want him to be just another stadium jumper driven by a poltergeist.

The bum rests on his back, that's easy enough, then add a foot. Next, we'll just connect the dots.

Add the head. Our rider is leaning forward, so I've added the oval lower.

Halfway there! Keep going!

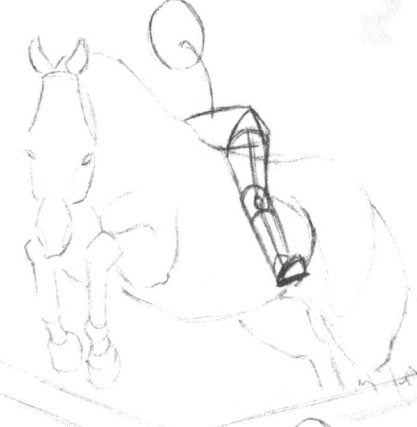

Build a body. Notice how the shoulders are raised up to the ears.

Add some arms, and you're done.

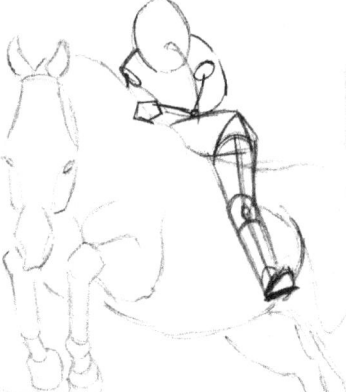

FIN!

Let's do another one. This time, we'll try a barrel racer.

I decided that I wanted to make our racer rounding the barrel, so the weight is on the outstretched foot.

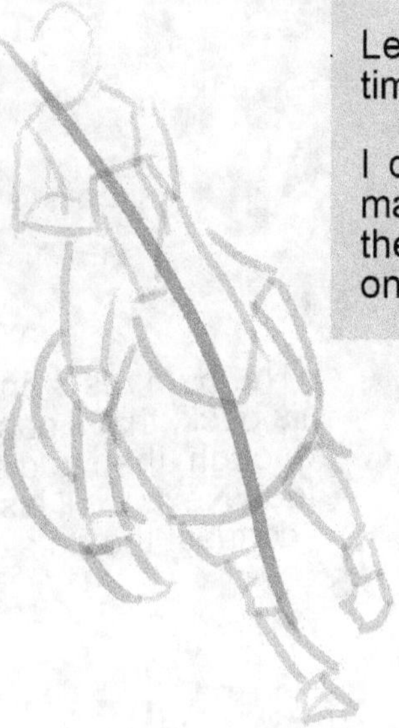

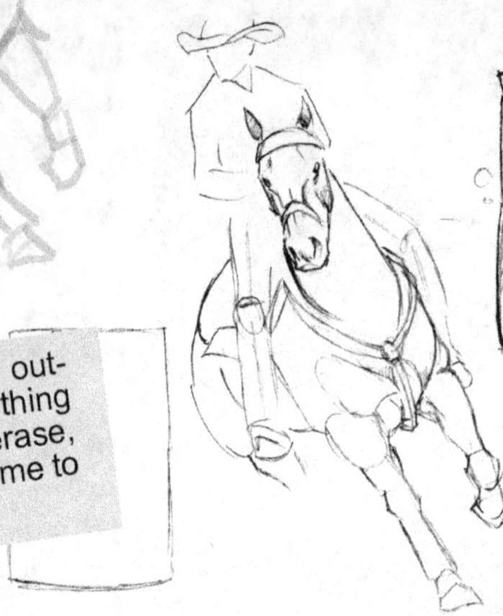

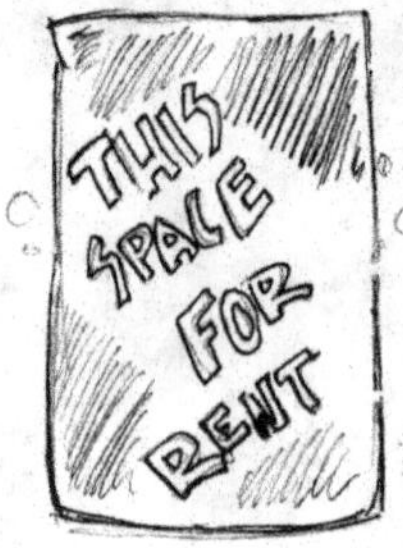

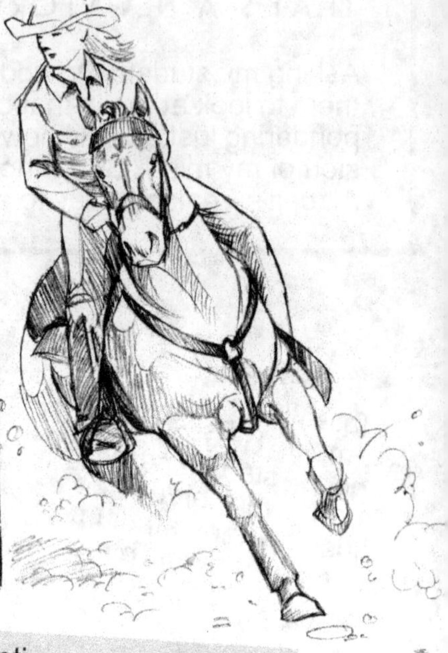

Now we add some outlines. If there's anything we want to add or erase, this is a really easy time to do it, and...

...continue your outlines and shadows until you're happy, or bored, with it.

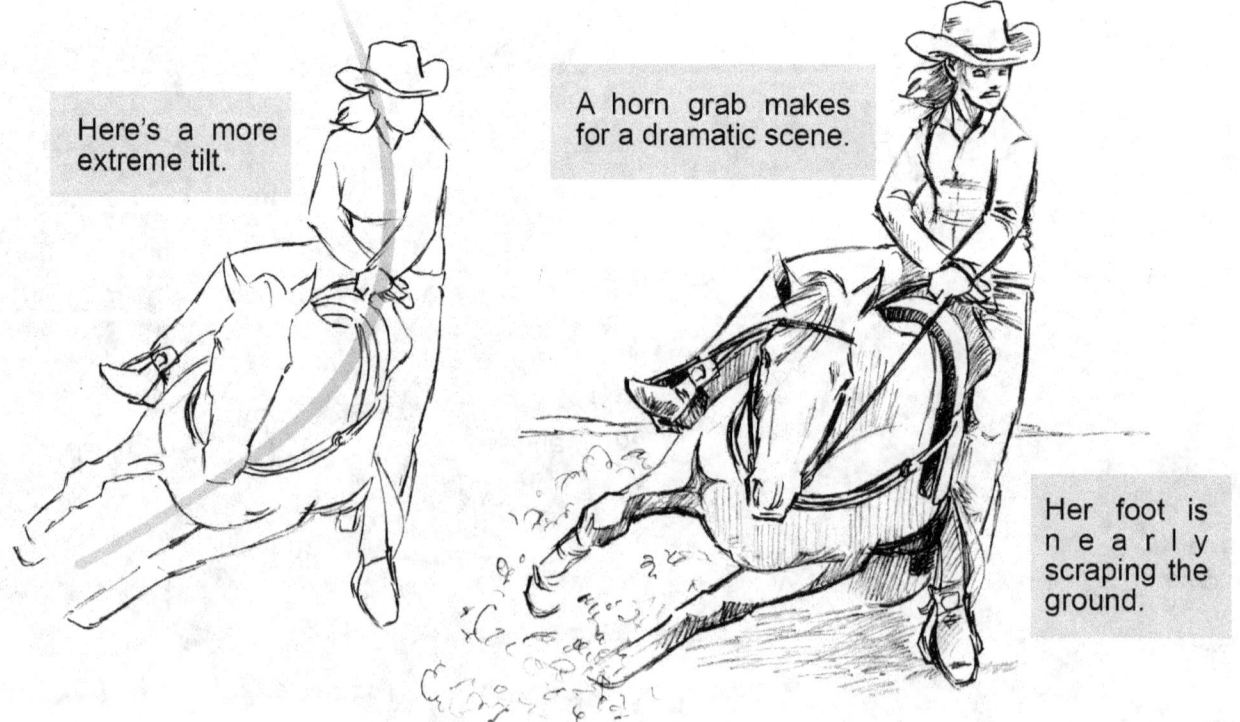

Here's a more extreme tilt.

A horn grab makes for a dramatic scene.

Her foot is n e a r l y scraping the ground.

SEQUENCE OF MOTIONS

You don't have to be a dedicated animator to understand movement or a licensed veterinarian to know the muscle and bones of an animal. Do you notice that the slope of the horse's face is parallel to the slope of their shoulders?

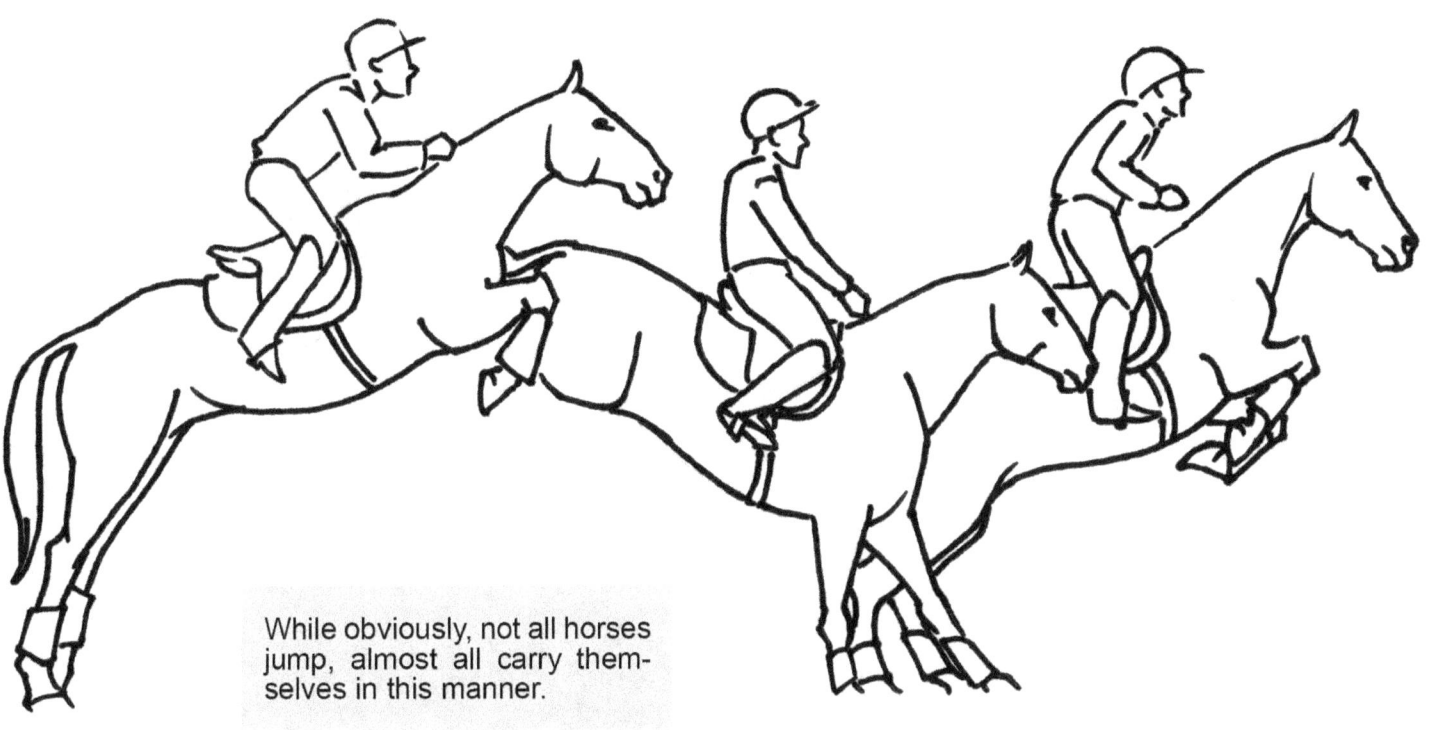

While obviously, not all horses jump, almost all carry themselves in this manner.

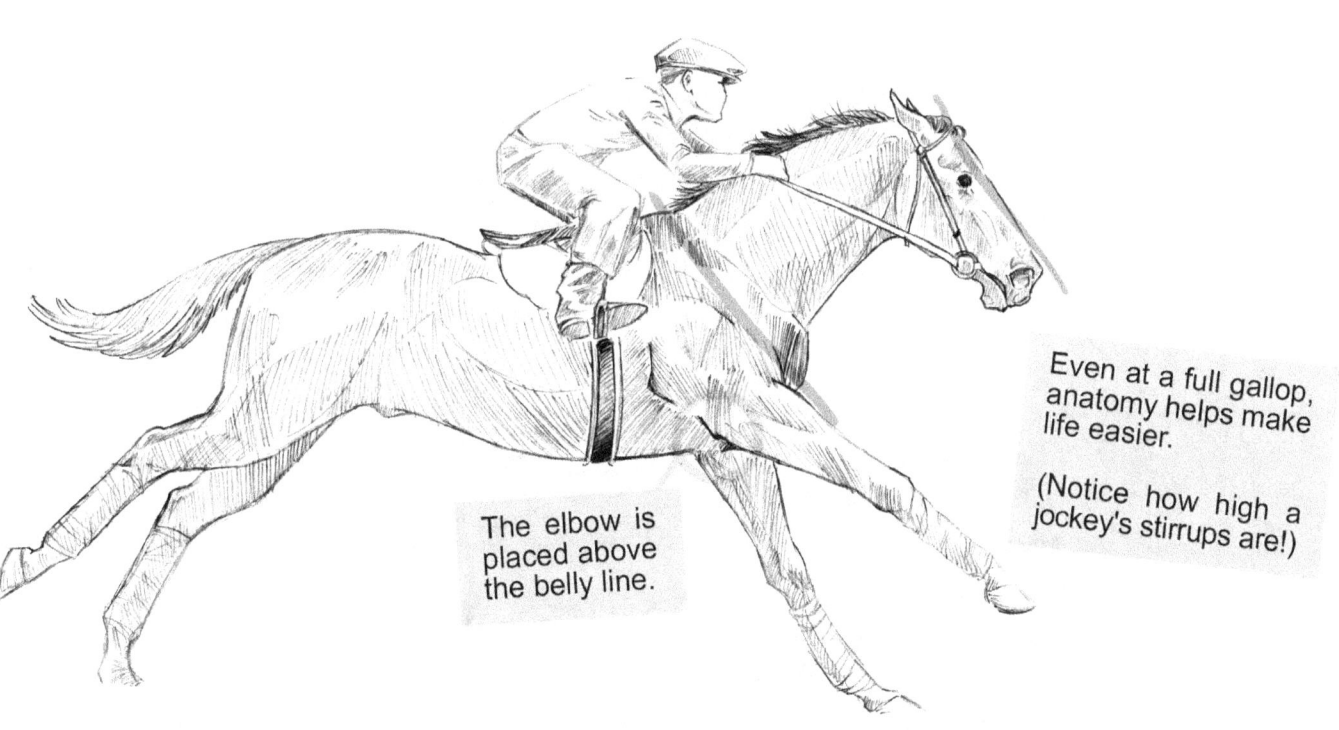

Even at a full gallop, anatomy helps make life easier.

(Notice how high a jockey's stirrups are!)

The elbow is placed above the belly line.

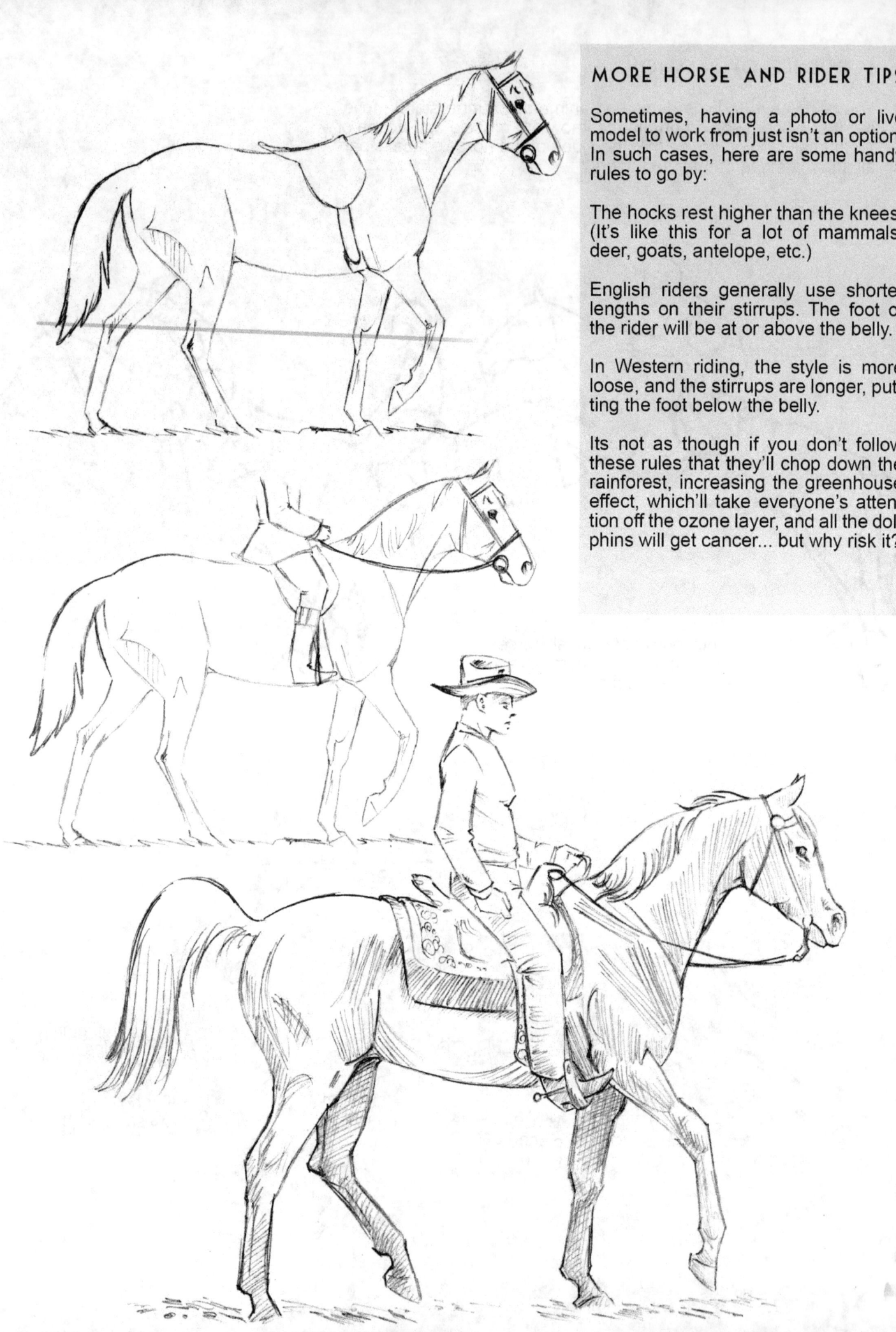

MORE HORSE AND RIDER TIPS

Sometimes, having a photo or live model to work from just isn't an option. In such cases, here are some handy rules to go by:

The hocks rest higher than the knees. (It's like this for a lot of mammals, deer, goats, antelope, etc.)

English riders generally use shorter lengths on their stirrups. The foot of the rider will be at or above the belly.

In Western riding, the style is more loose, and the stirrups are longer, putting the foot below the belly.

Its not as though if you don't follow these rules that they'll chop down the rainforest, increasing the greenhouse effect, which'll take everyone's attention off the ozone layer, and all the dolphins will get cancer... but why risk it?

ACTION MADE EASY

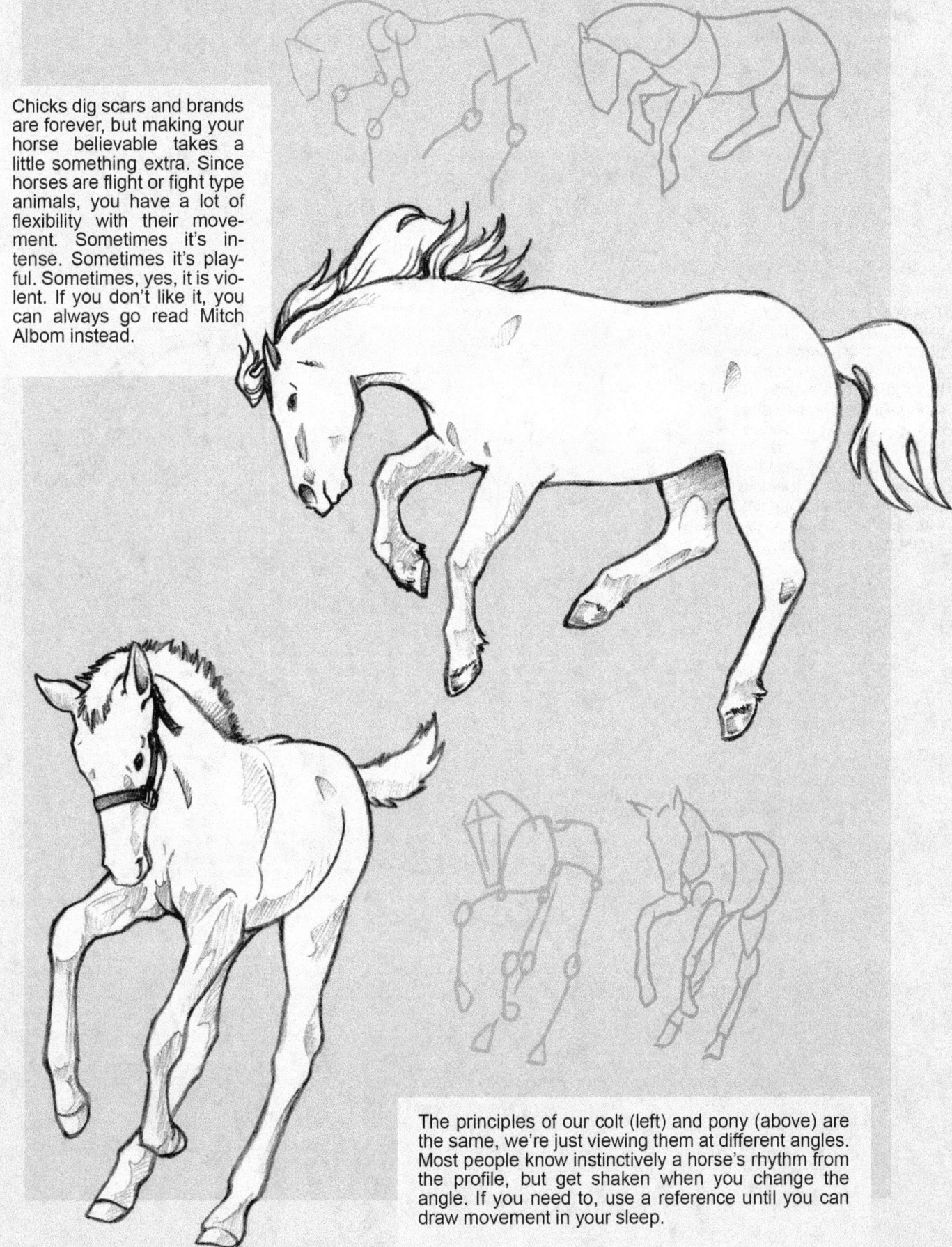

Chicks dig scars and brands are forever, but making your horse believable takes a little something extra. Since horses are flight or fight type animals, you have a lot of flexibility with their movement. Sometimes it's intense. Sometimes it's playful. Sometimes, yes, it is violent. If you don't like it, you can always go read Mitch Albom instead.

The principles of our colt (left) and pony (above) are the same, we're just viewing them at different angles. Most people know instinctively a horse's rhythm from the profile, but get shaken when you change the angle. If you need to, use a reference until you can draw movement in your sleep.

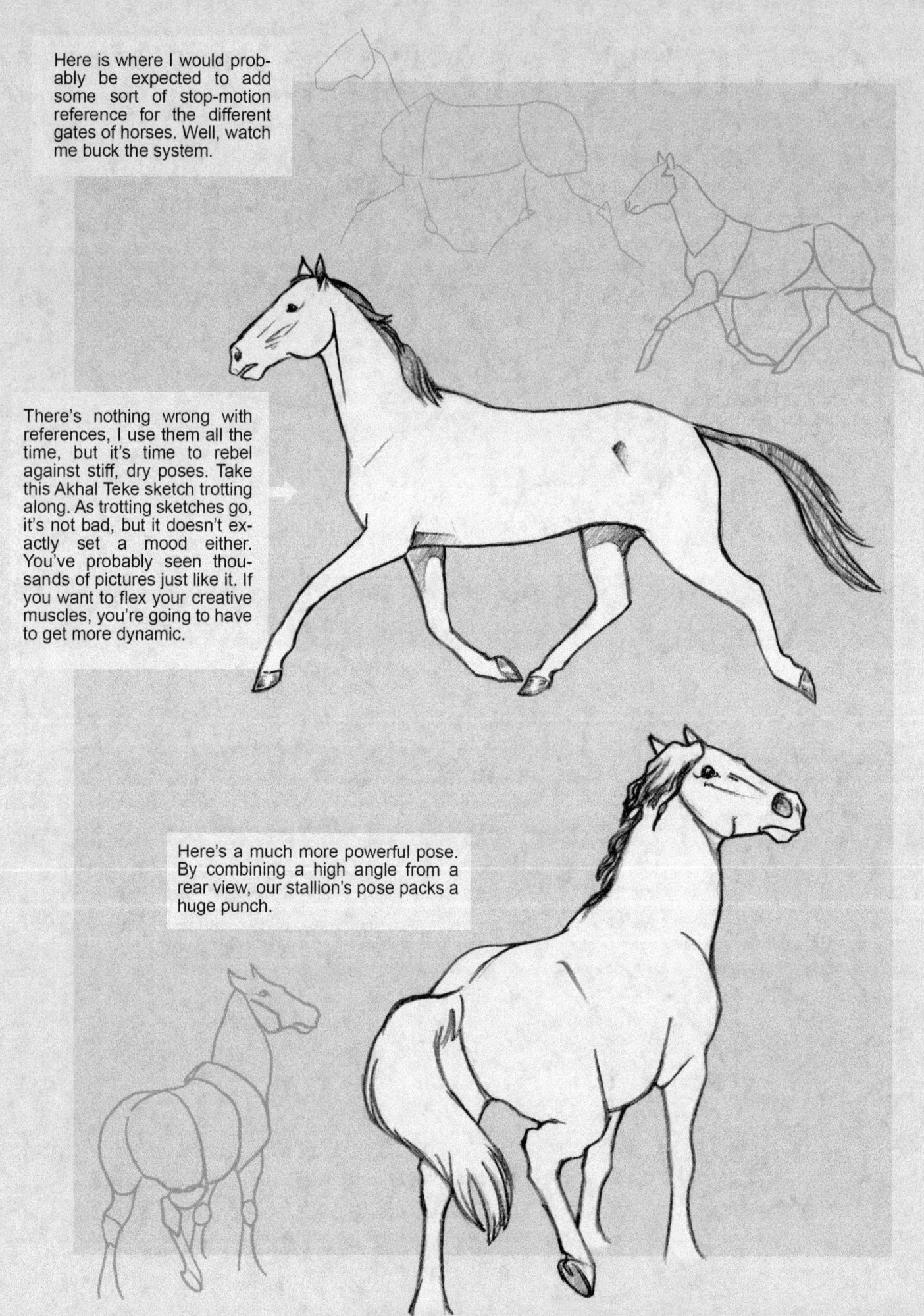

Here is where I would probably be expected to add some sort of stop-motion reference for the different gates of horses. Well, watch me buck the system.

There's nothing wrong with references, I use them all the time, but it's time to rebel against stiff, dry poses. Take this Akhal Teke sketch trotting along. As trotting sketches go, it's not bad, but it doesn't exactly set a mood either. You've probably seen thousands of pictures just like it. If you want to flex your creative muscles, you're going to have to get more dynamic.

Here's a much more powerful pose. By combining a high angle from a rear view, our stallion's pose packs a huge punch.

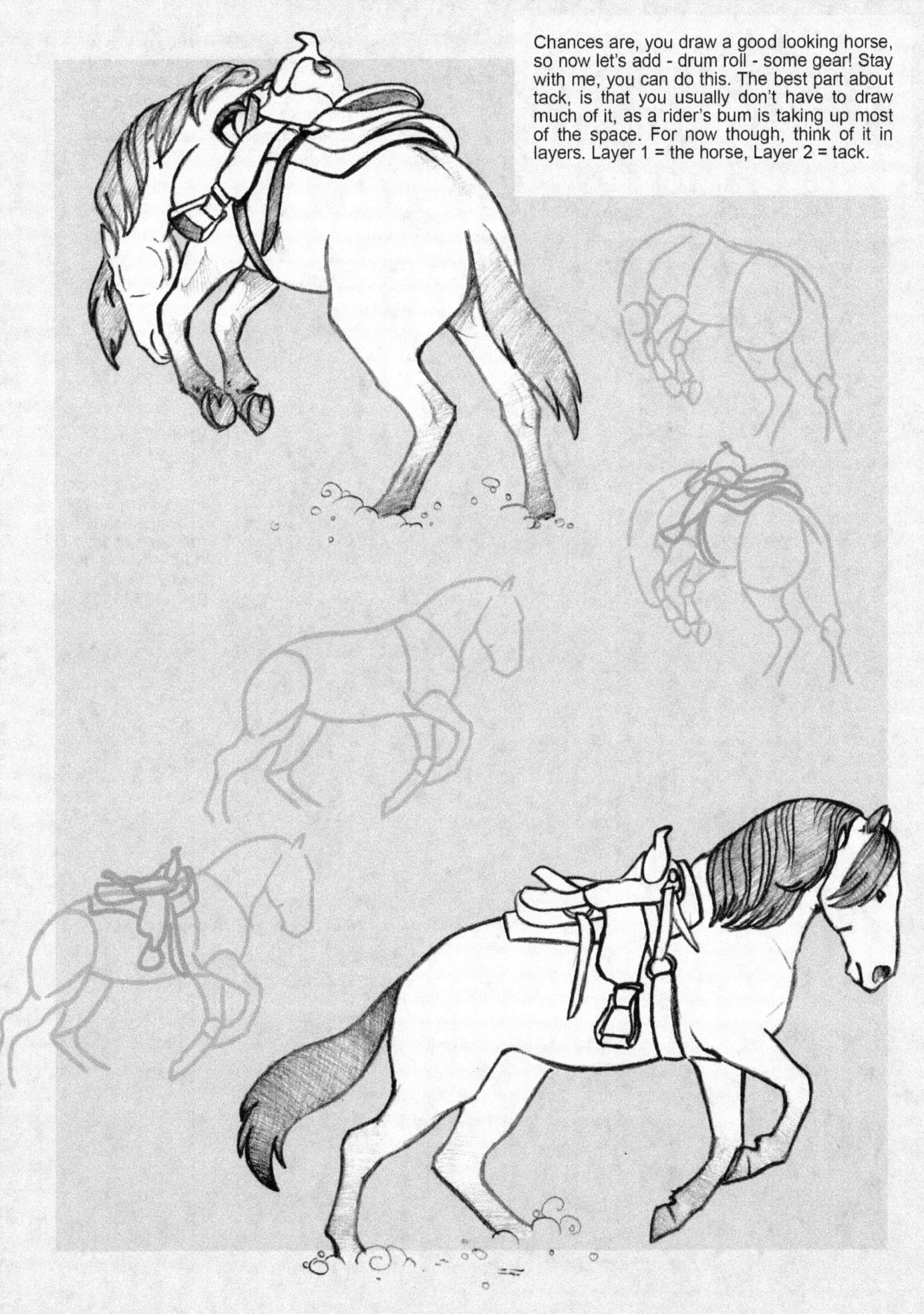

Chances are, you draw a good looking horse, so now let's add - drum roll - some gear! Stay with me, you can do this. The best part about tack, is that you usually don't have to draw much of it, as a rider's bum is taking up most of the space. For now though, think of it in layers. Layer 1 = the horse, Layer 2 = tack.

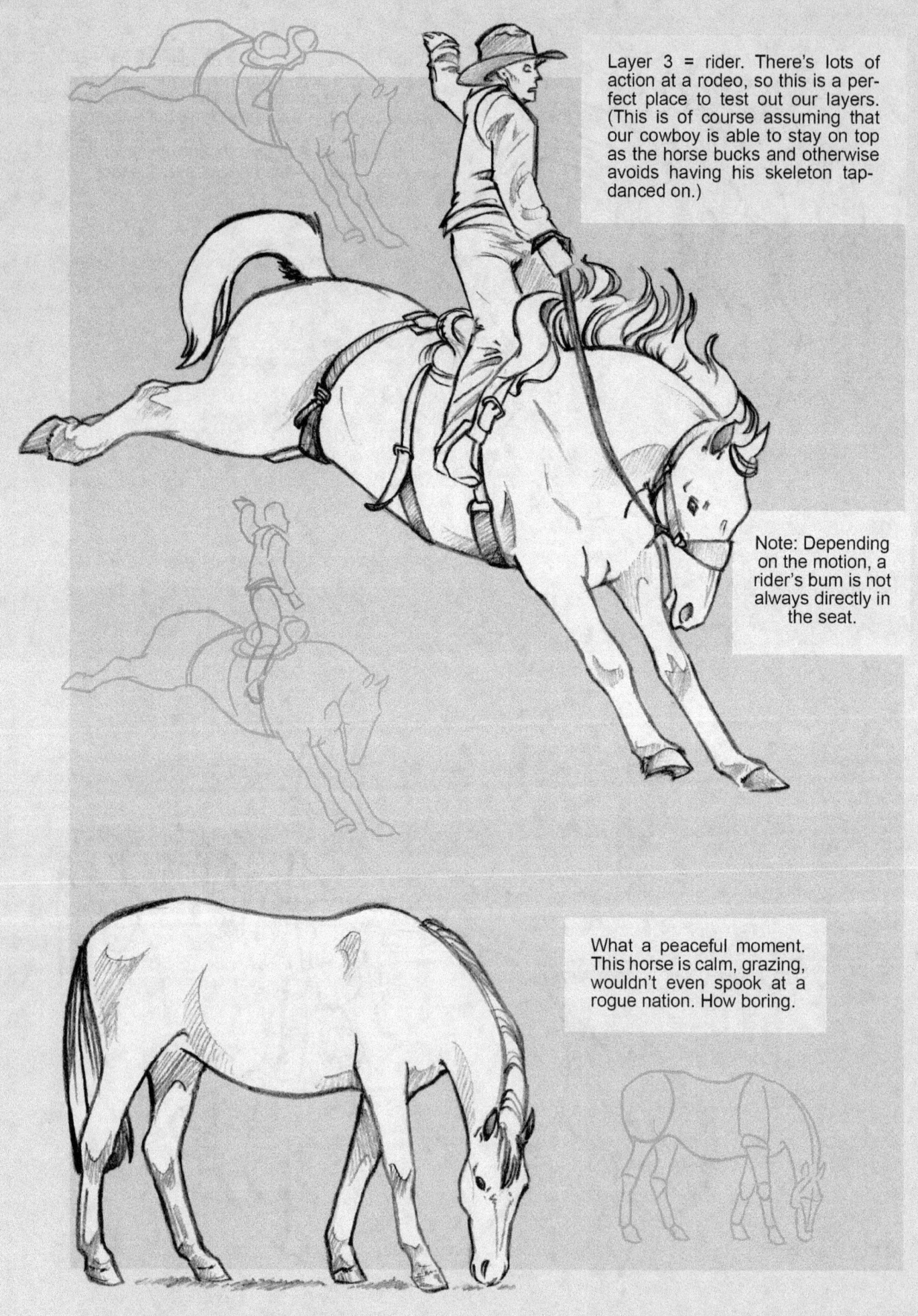

Layer 3 = rider. There's lots of action at a rodeo, so this is a perfect place to test out our layers. (This is of course assuming that our cowboy is able to stay on top as the horse bucks and otherwise avoids having his skeleton tap-danced on.)

Note: Depending on the motion, a rider's bum is not always directly in the seat.

What a peaceful moment. This horse is calm, grazing, wouldn't even spook at a rogue nation. How boring.

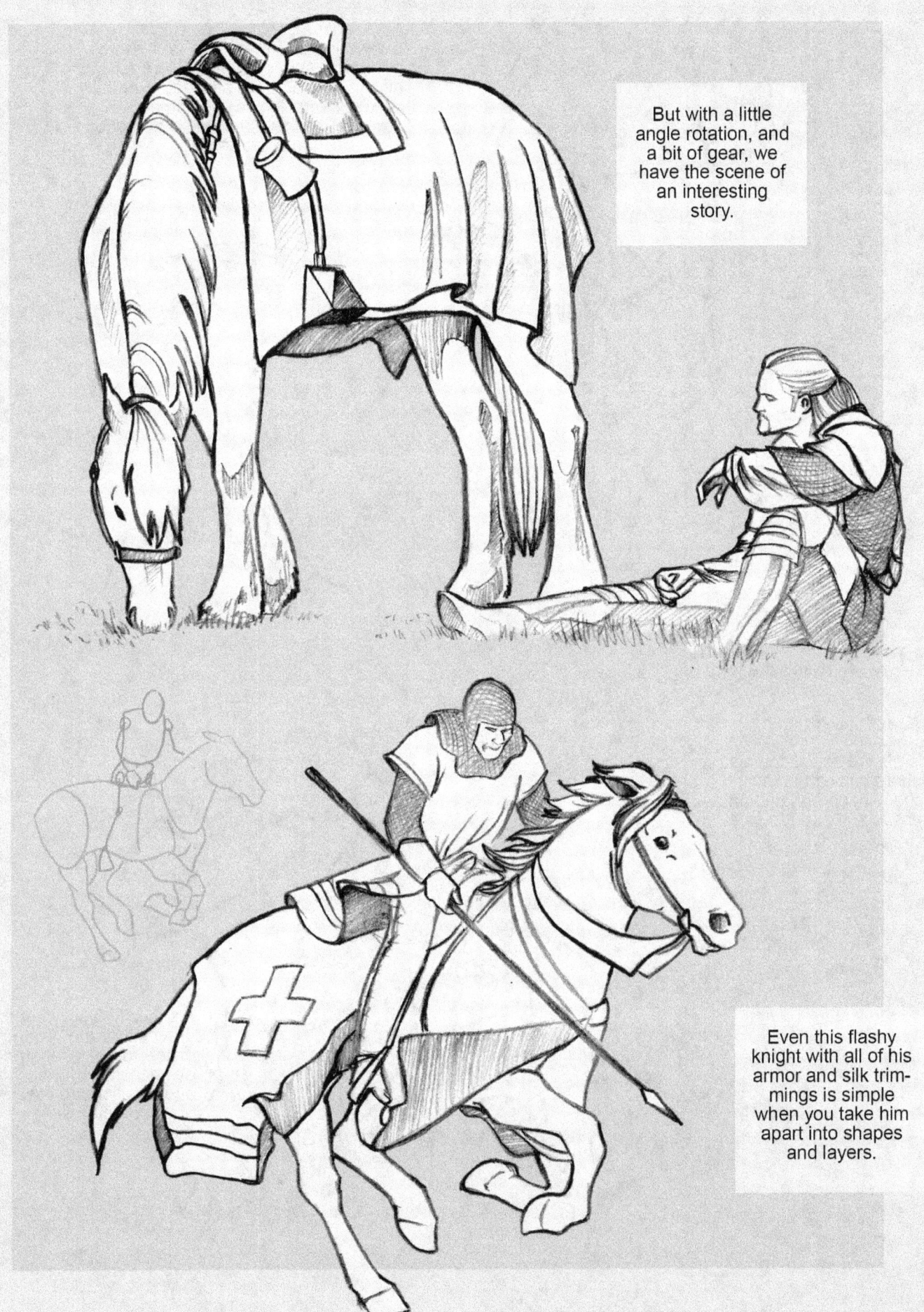

But with a little angle rotation, and a bit of gear, we have the scene of an interesting story.

Even this flashy knight with all of his armor and silk trimmings is simple when you take him apart into shapes and layers.

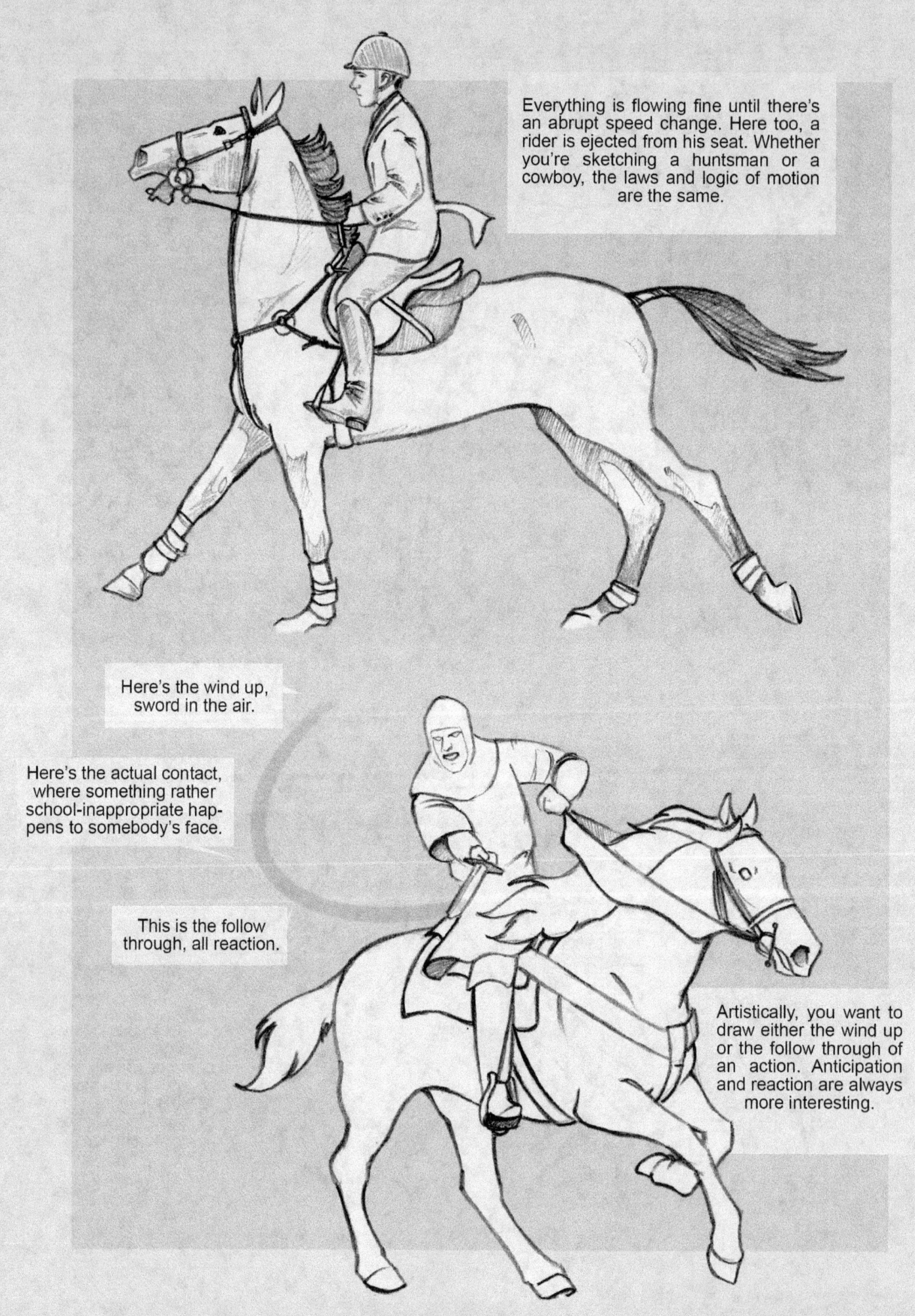

Everything is flowing fine until there's an abrupt speed change. Here too, a rider is ejected from his seat. Whether you're sketching a huntsman or a cowboy, the laws and logic of motion are the same.

Here's the wind up, sword in the air.

Here's the actual contact, where something rather school-inappropriate happens to somebody's face.

This is the follow through, all reaction.

Artistically, you want to draw either the wind up or the follow through of an action. Anticipation and reaction are always more interesting.

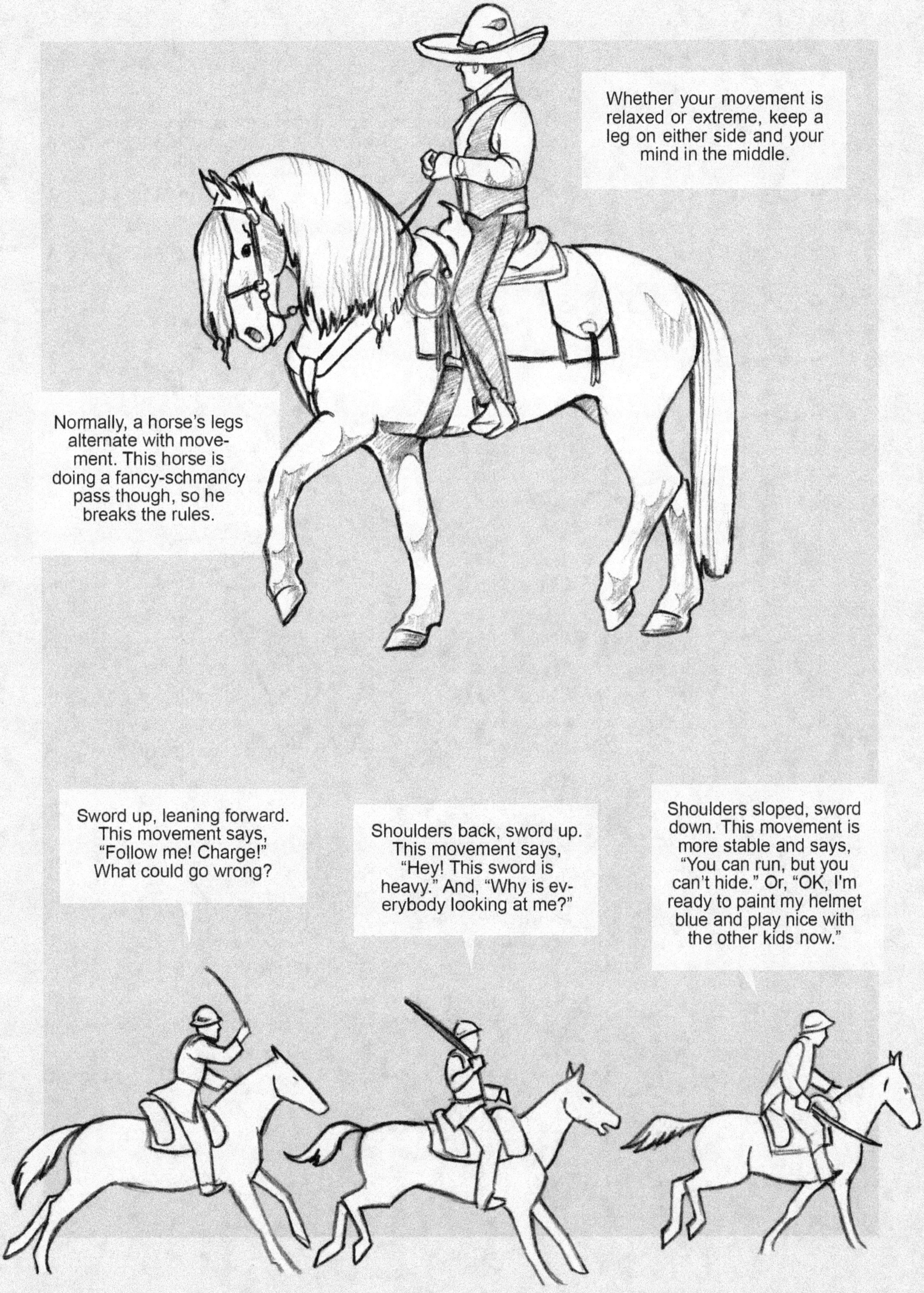

Whether your movement is relaxed or extreme, keep a leg on either side and your mind in the middle.

Normally, a horse's legs alternate with movement. This horse is doing a fancy-schmancy pass though, so he breaks the rules.

Sword up, leaning forward. This movement says, "Follow me! Charge!" What could go wrong?

Shoulders back, sword up. This movement says, "Hey! This sword is heavy." And, "Why is everybody looking at me?"

Shoulders sloped, sword down. This movement is more stable and says, "You can run, but you can't hide." Or, "OK, I'm ready to paint my helmet blue and play nice with the other kids now."

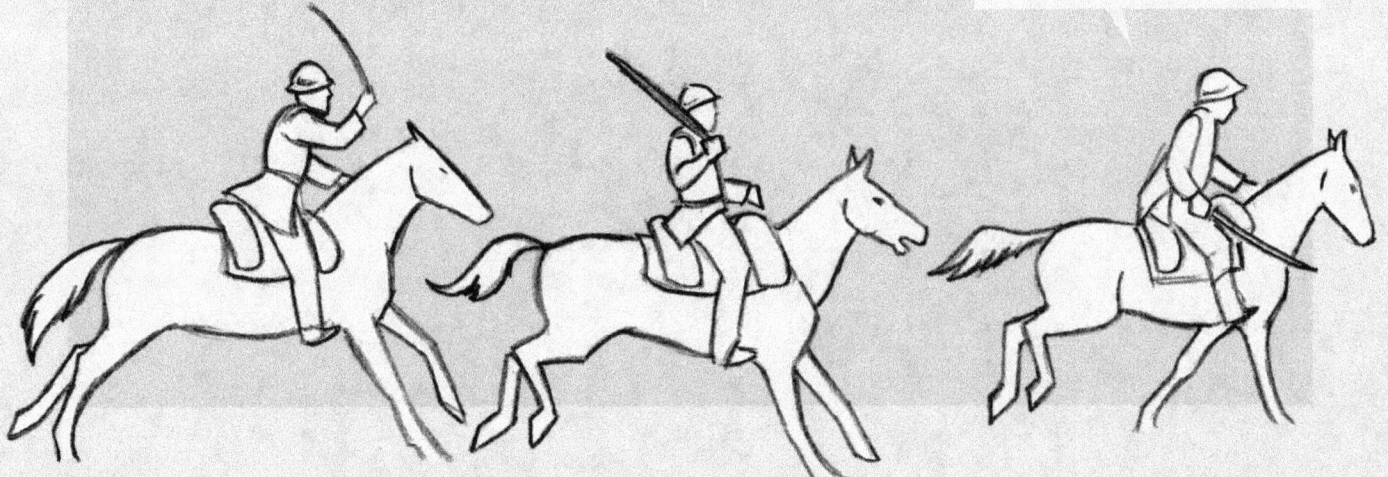

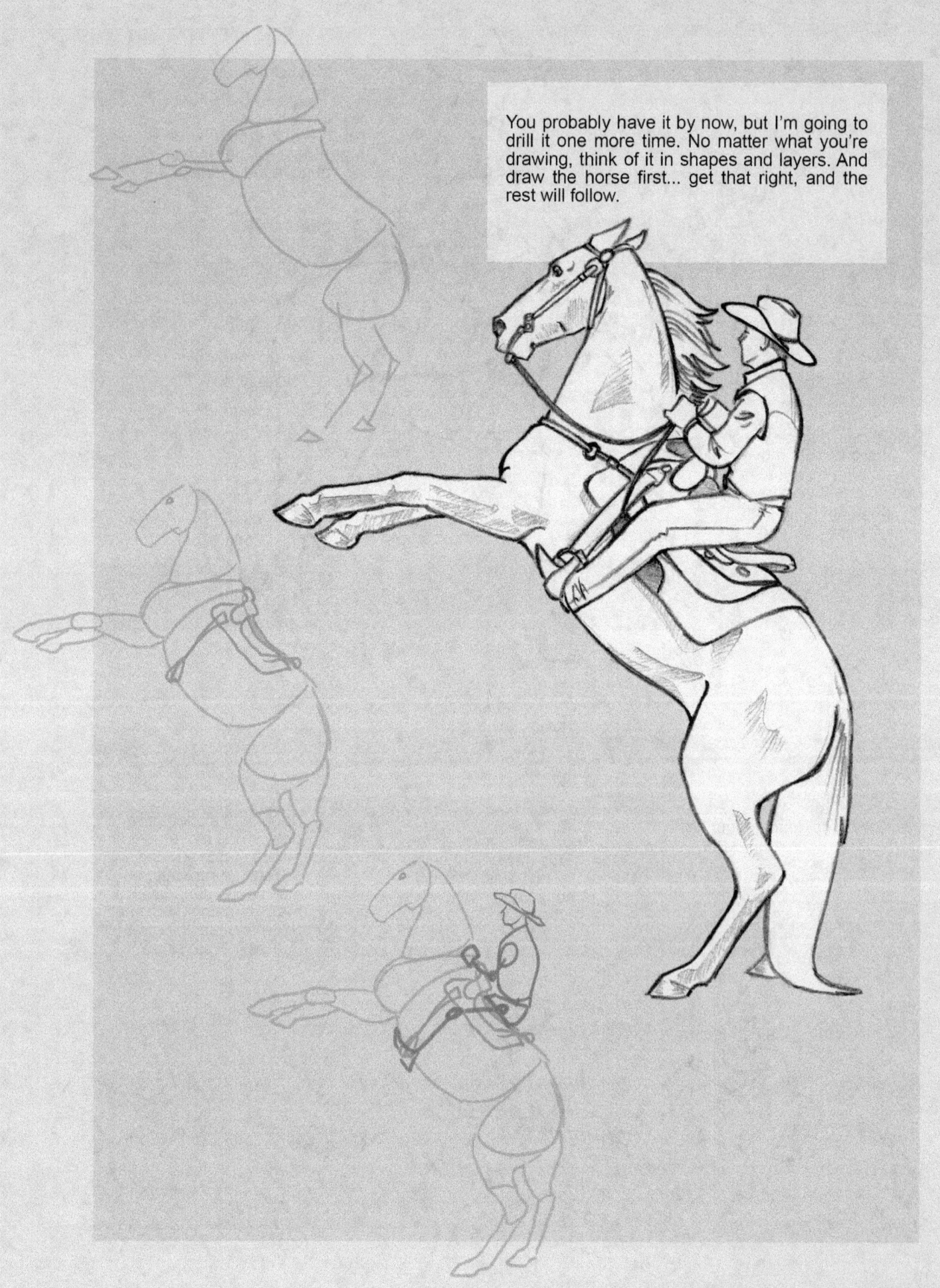

You probably have it by now, but I'm going to drill it one more time. No matter what you're drawing, think of it in shapes and layers. And draw the horse first... get that right, and the rest will follow.

OBEY GRAVITY

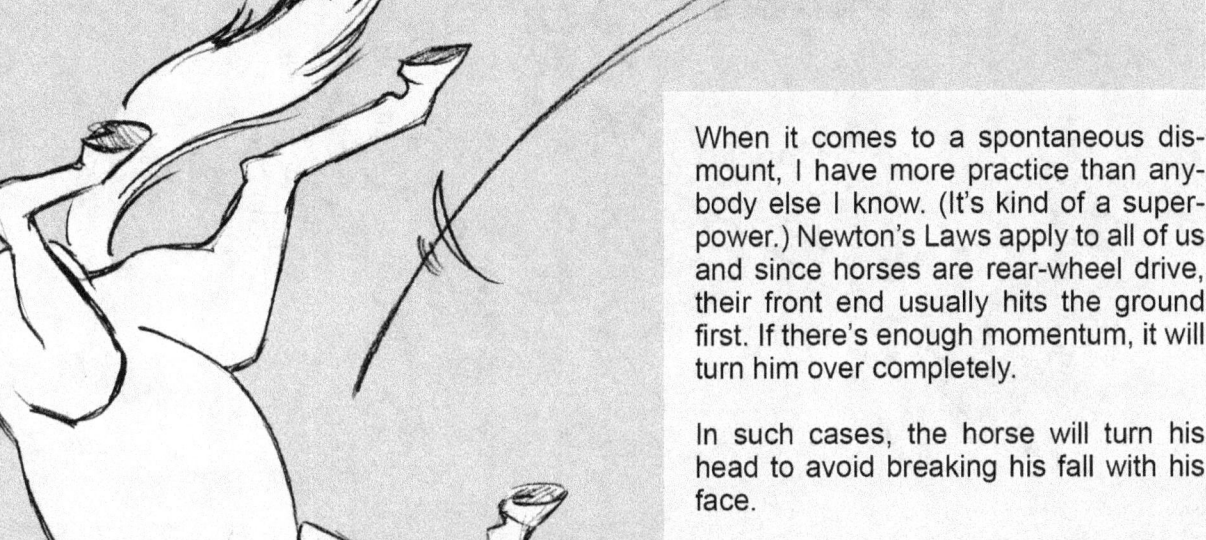

When it comes to a spontaneous dis-mount, I have more practice than any-body else I know. (It's kind of a super-power.) Newton's Laws apply to all of us and since horses are rear-wheel drive, their front end usually hits the ground first. If there's enough momentum, it will turn him over completely.

In such cases, the horse will turn his head to avoid breaking his fall with his face.

I wish I could say I was always that smart.

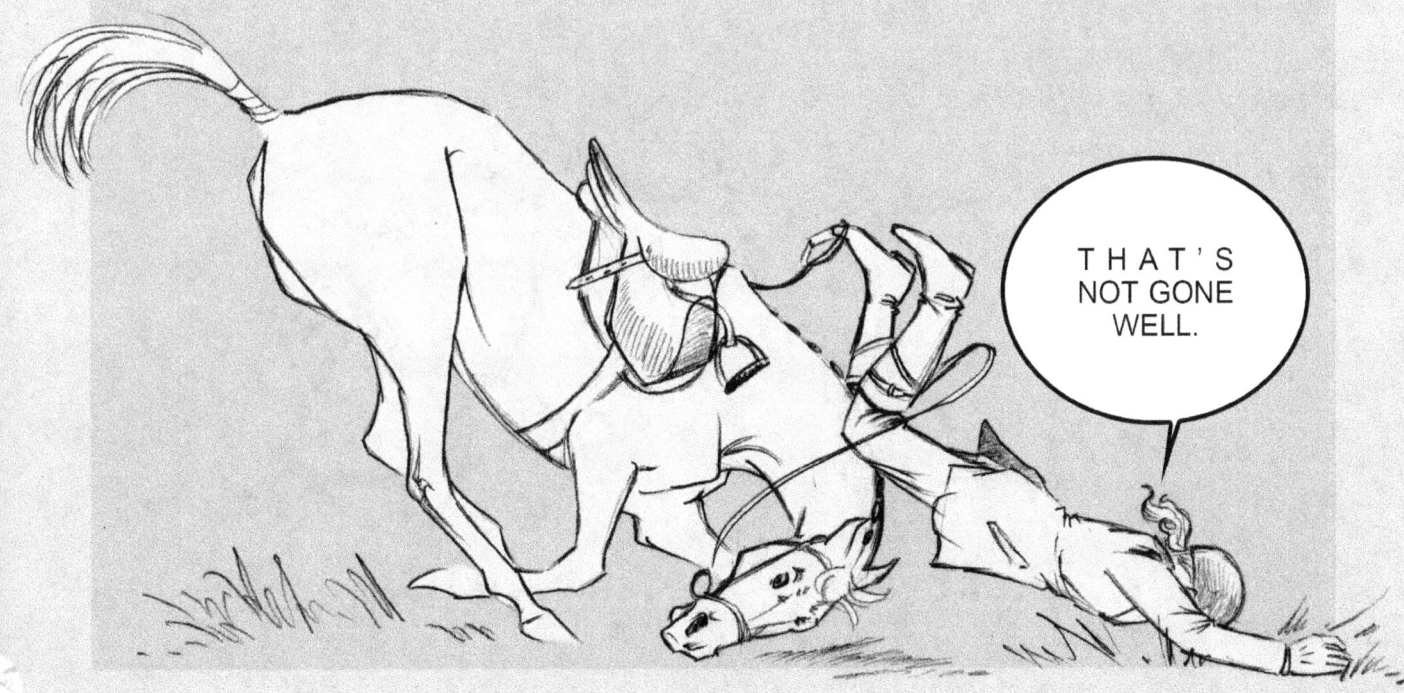

THAT'S NOT GONE WELL.

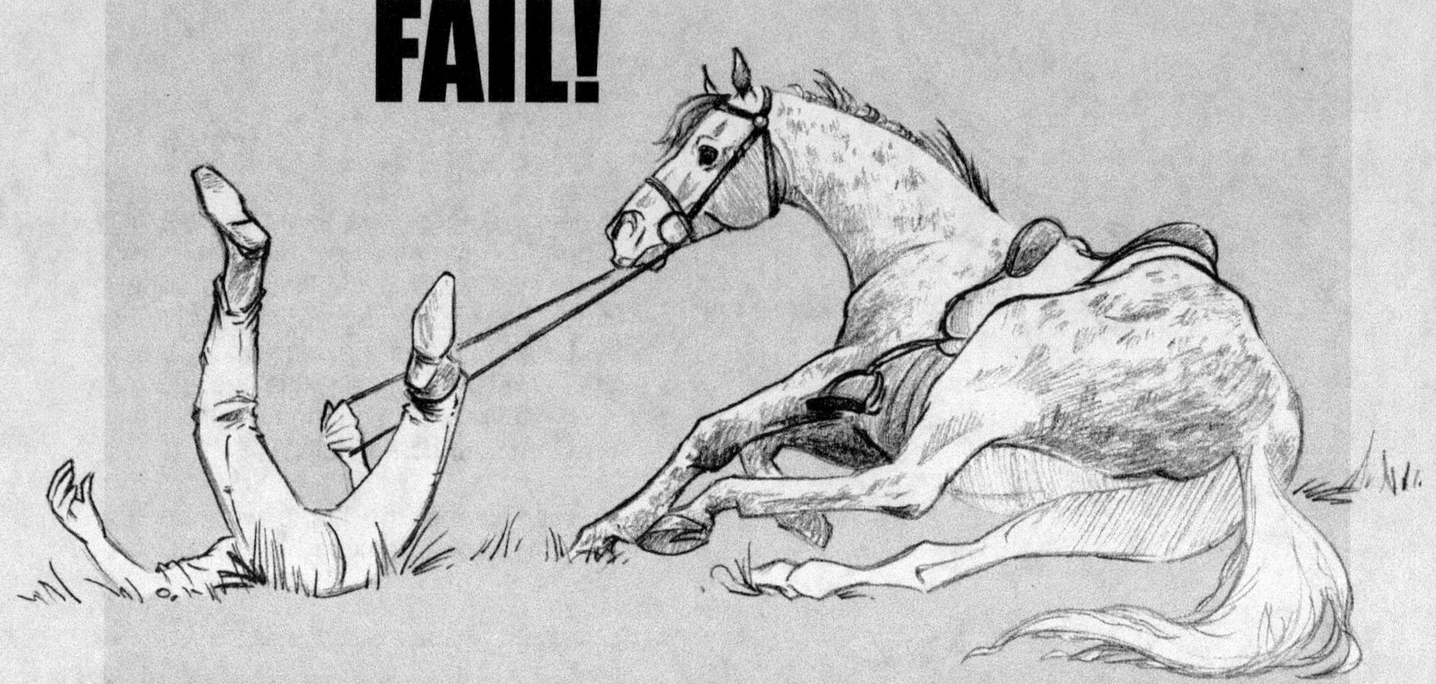

FAIL!

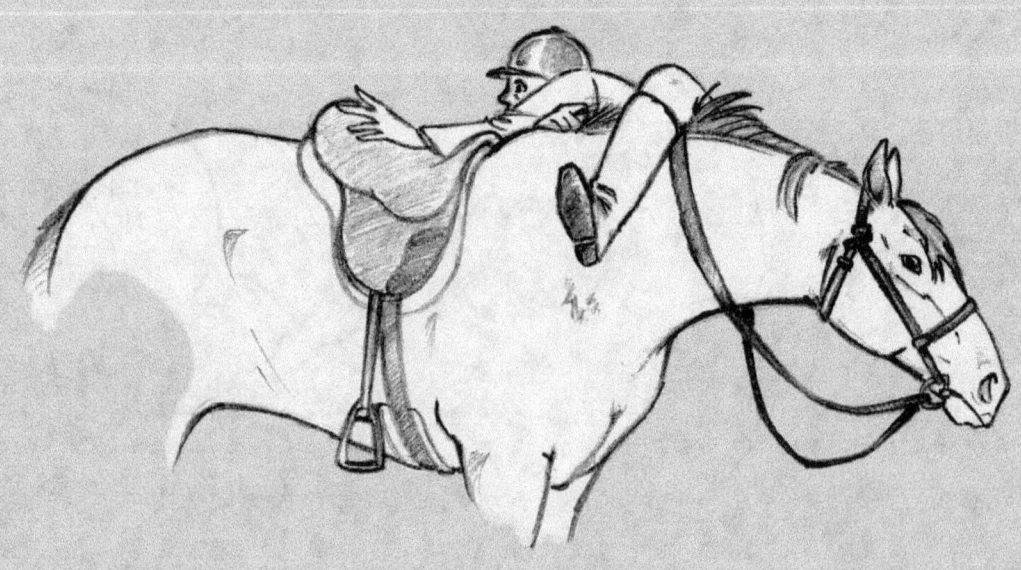

Of course, as with learning to do anything, cut yourself some slack. Not even the pros are perfect, so keep at it. Take the compliments with style, and knowing the great artist you are, you're going to have to handle a lot of compliments. And above all, even when it doesn't work out the way you planed... keep getting back on.

JUMPING

There is a mysterious fascination about jumping. It's not anything I can explain, but if you have any pride at all, consider yourself forewarned, steer clear of the jumping trials.

Proportionally, our horse and rider are sound, but its not a very interesting pose.

The view gives the sense of being eye-level with this subject. Possible, but highly unlikely if these are 2 meter jumps.

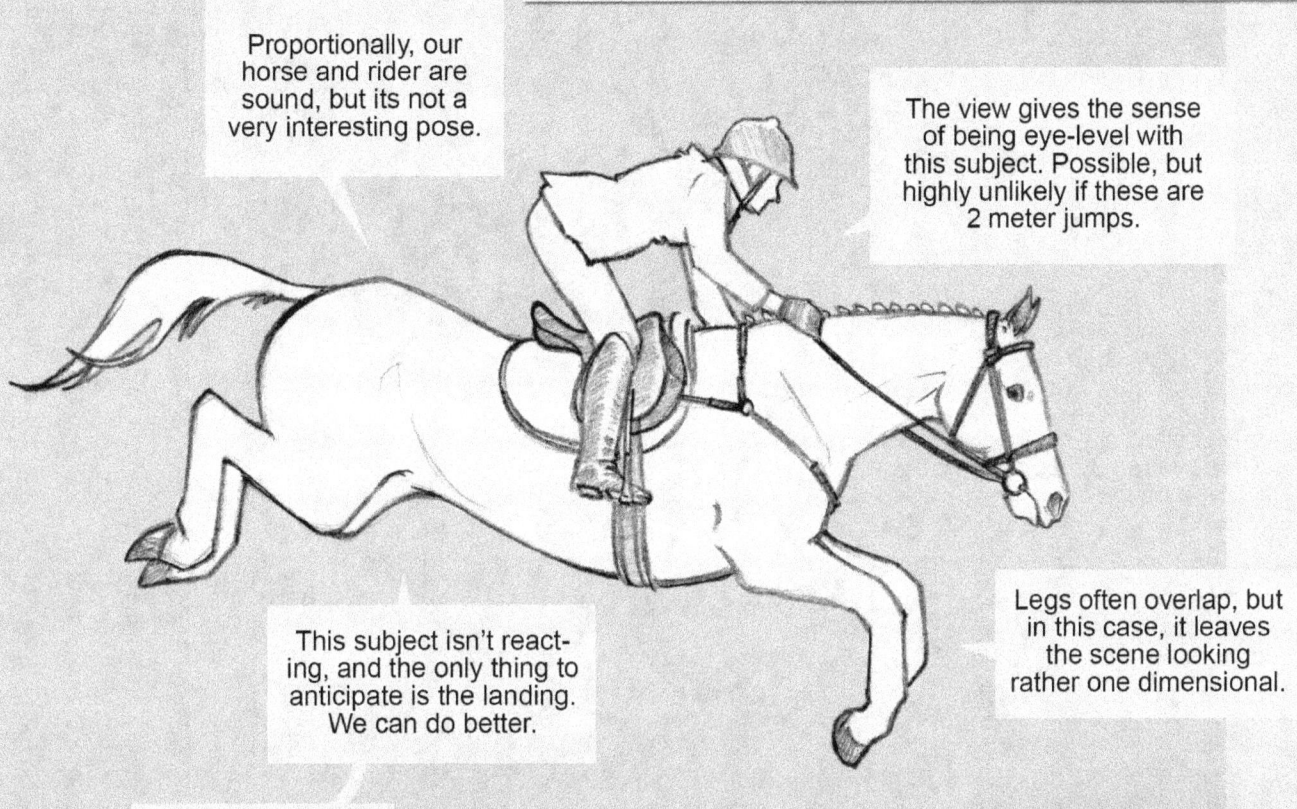

This subject isn't reacting, and the only thing to anticipate is the landing. We can do better.

Legs often overlap, but in this case, it leaves the scene looking rather one dimensional.

That's more like it!

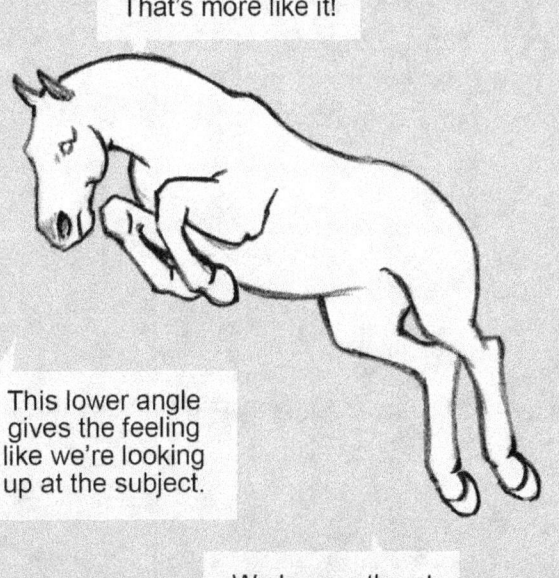

This lower angle gives the feeling like we're looking up at the subject.

We have a thrust of action from below taking us upwards and onwards!

RIDER TIPS

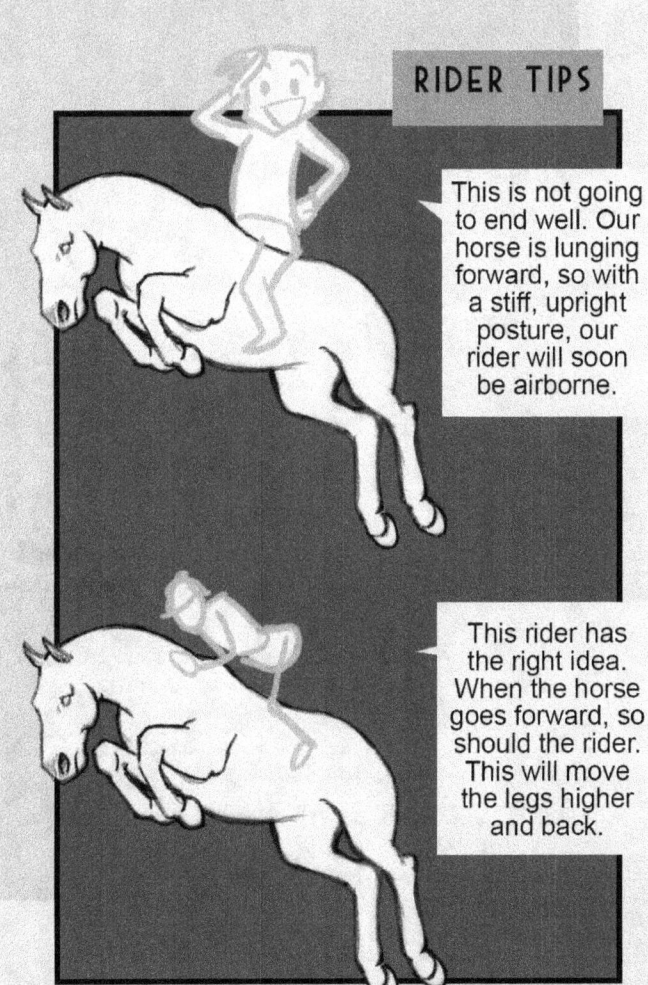

This is not going to end well. Our horse is lunging forward, so with a stiff, upright posture, our rider will soon be airborne.

This rider has the right idea. When the horse goes forward, so should the rider. This will move the legs higher and back.

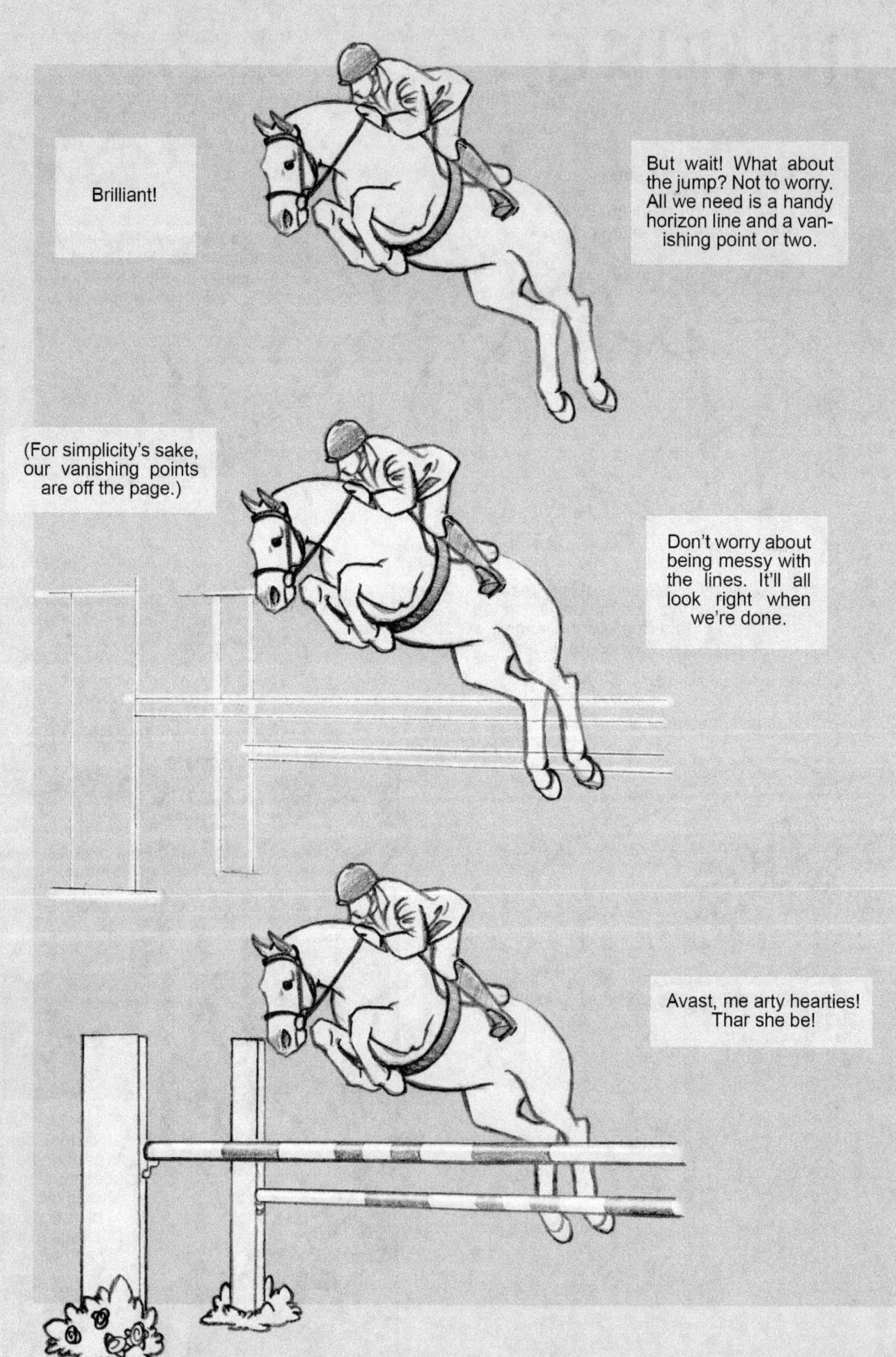

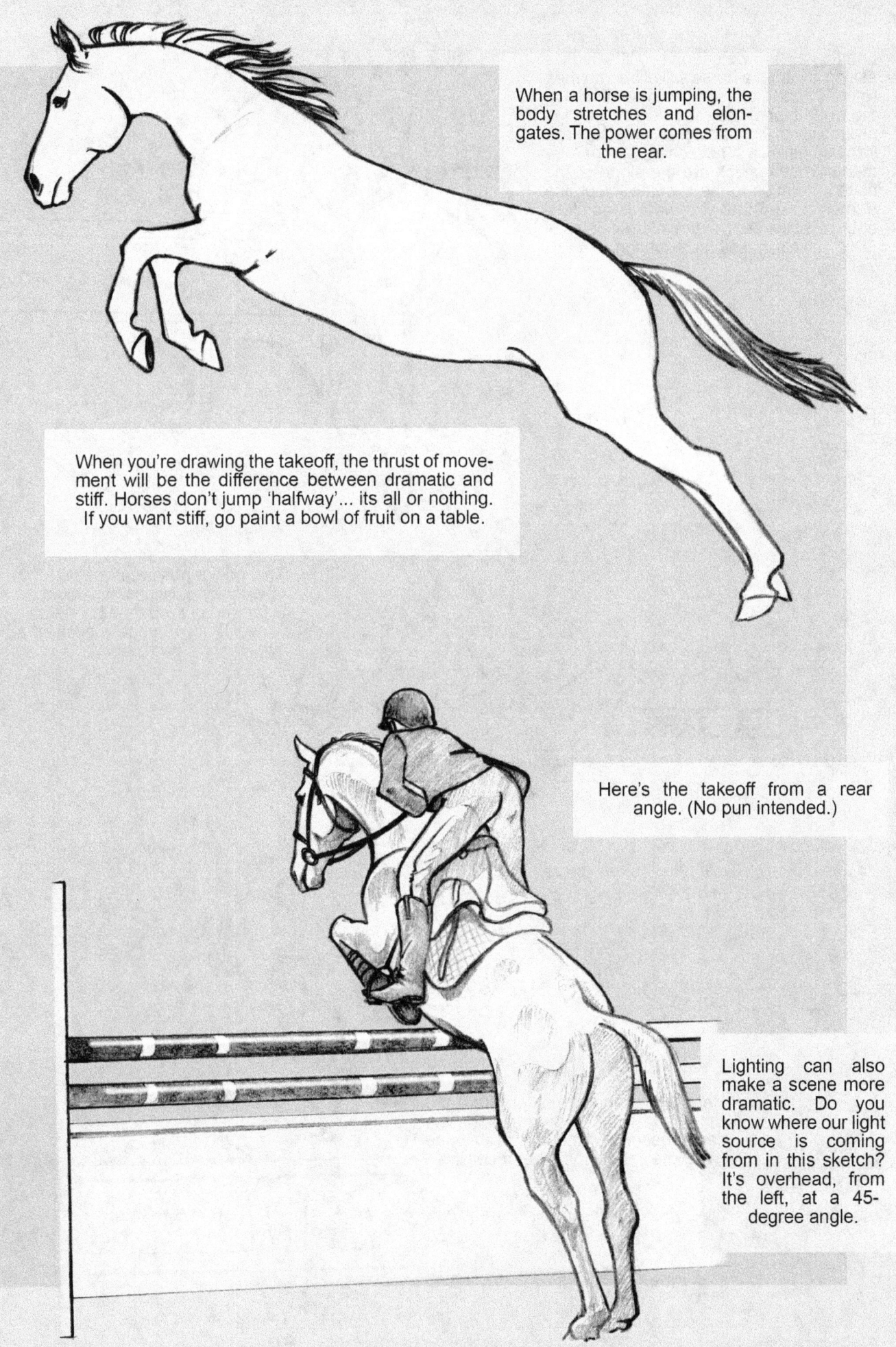

When a horse is jumping, the body stretches and elongates. The power comes from the rear.

When you're drawing the takeoff, the thrust of movement will be the difference between dramatic and stiff. Horses don't jump 'halfway'... its all or nothing. If you want stiff, go paint a bowl of fruit on a table.

Here's the takeoff from a rear angle. (No pun intended.)

Lighting can also make a scene more dramatic. Do you know where our light source is coming from in this sketch? It's overhead, from the left, at a 45-degree angle.

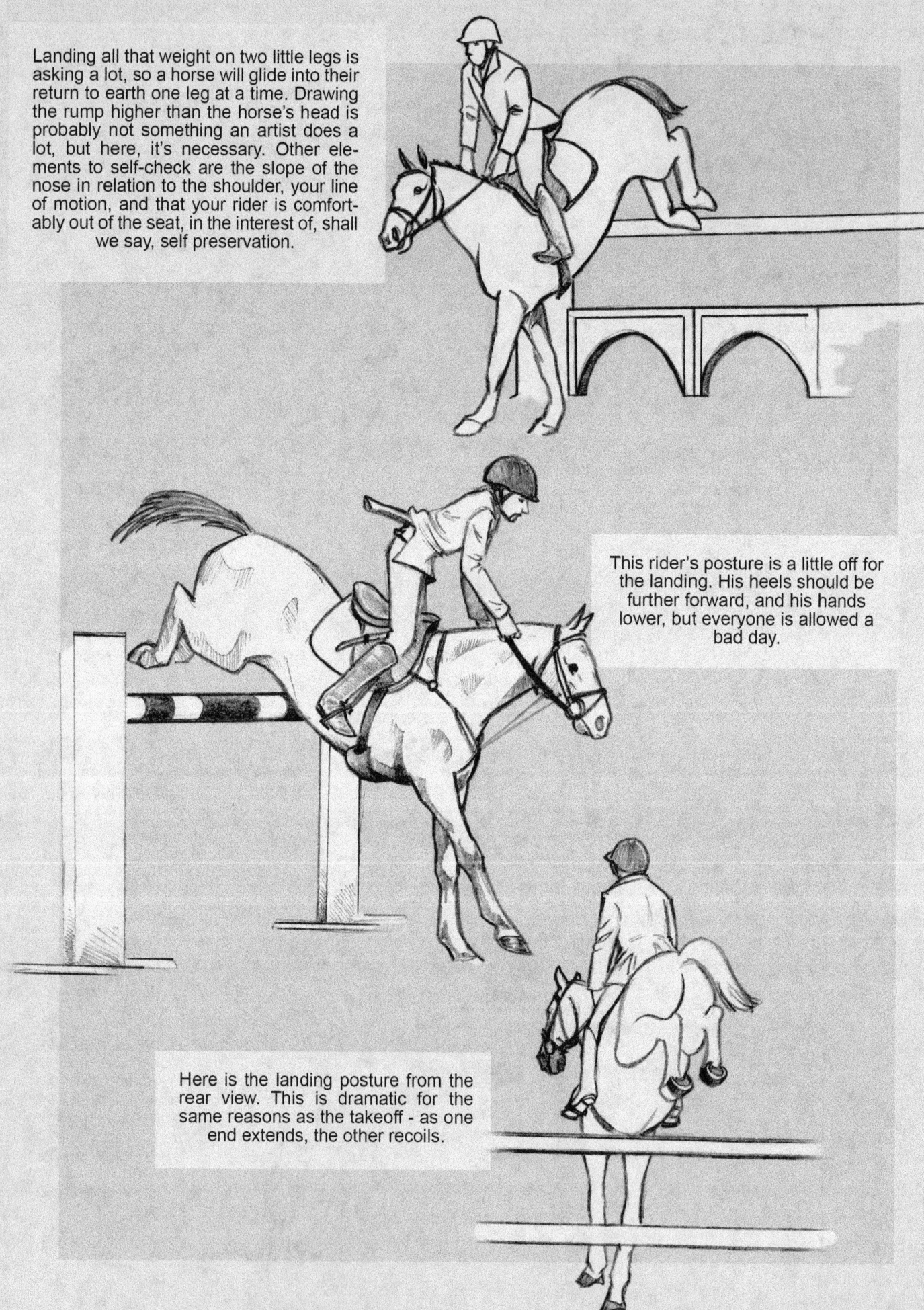

Landing all that weight on two little legs is asking a lot, so a horse will glide into their return to earth one leg at a time. Drawing the rump higher than the horse's head is probably not something an artist does a lot, but here, it's necessary. Other elements to self-check are the slope of the nose in relation to the shoulder, your line of motion, and that your rider is comfortably out of the seat, in the interest of, shall we say, self preservation.

This rider's posture is a little off for the landing. His heels should be further forward, and his hands lower, but everyone is allowed a bad day.

Here is the landing posture from the rear view. This is dramatic for the same reasons as the takeoff - as one end extends, the other recoils.

HORSE POWER

Gentle giants, steady workers, and hay burners, horsepower was the way people got things done for thousands of years. Without horses, Alexander the Great could not have swept across Asia, the battles of Kawanakajima in Japan could have turned out very differently, and Paul Revere would never have been able to make his famous ride, from village to dell, shouting, "I CAN'T STOP MY HORSE!"

Regardless of where or when, horses have had a major impact on humanity and vice versa. Here are some of the breeds in action with accurate information, along with some historical anecdotes which are not, because I just made them up.

If you ever wondered if horses were rear-wheel-drive, look no further than this Belgian team. Since weight-pulls are done in a straight line, understeer isn't so much of a problem.

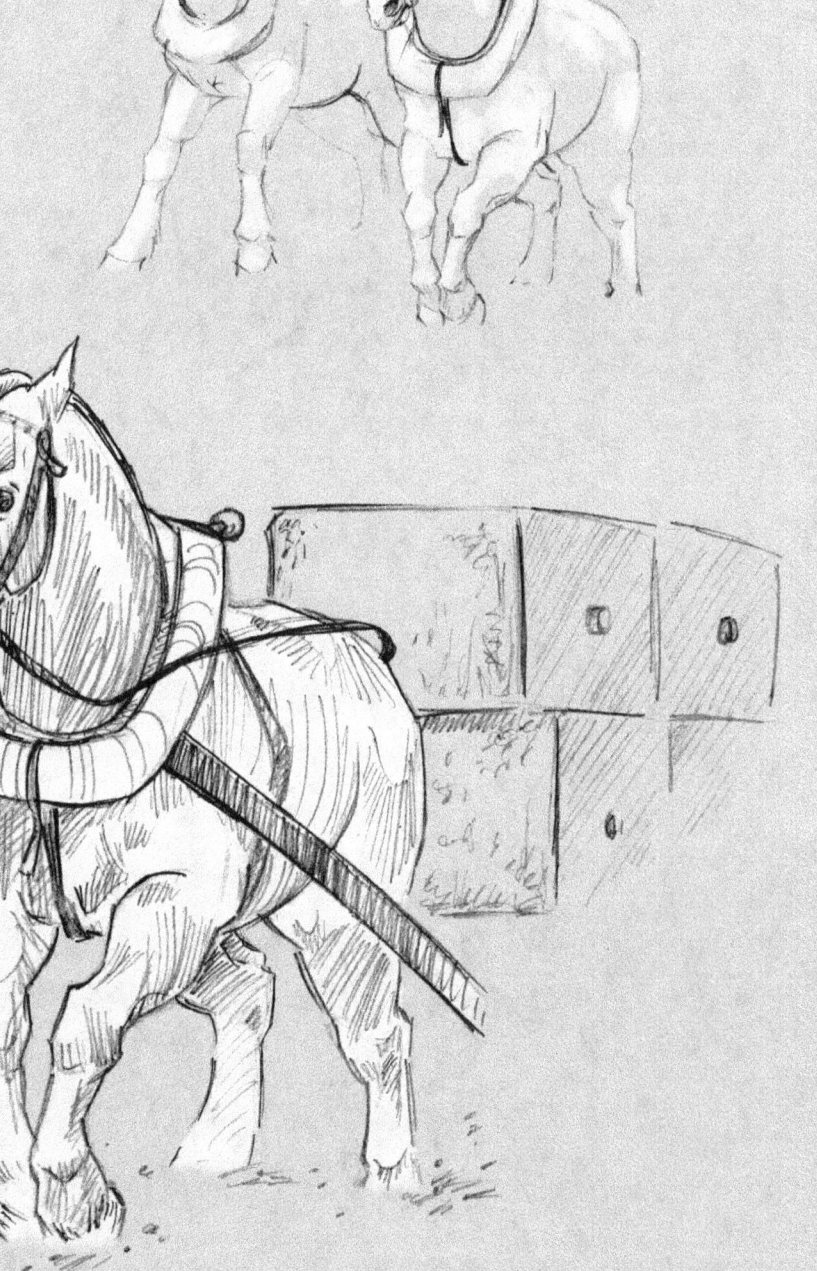

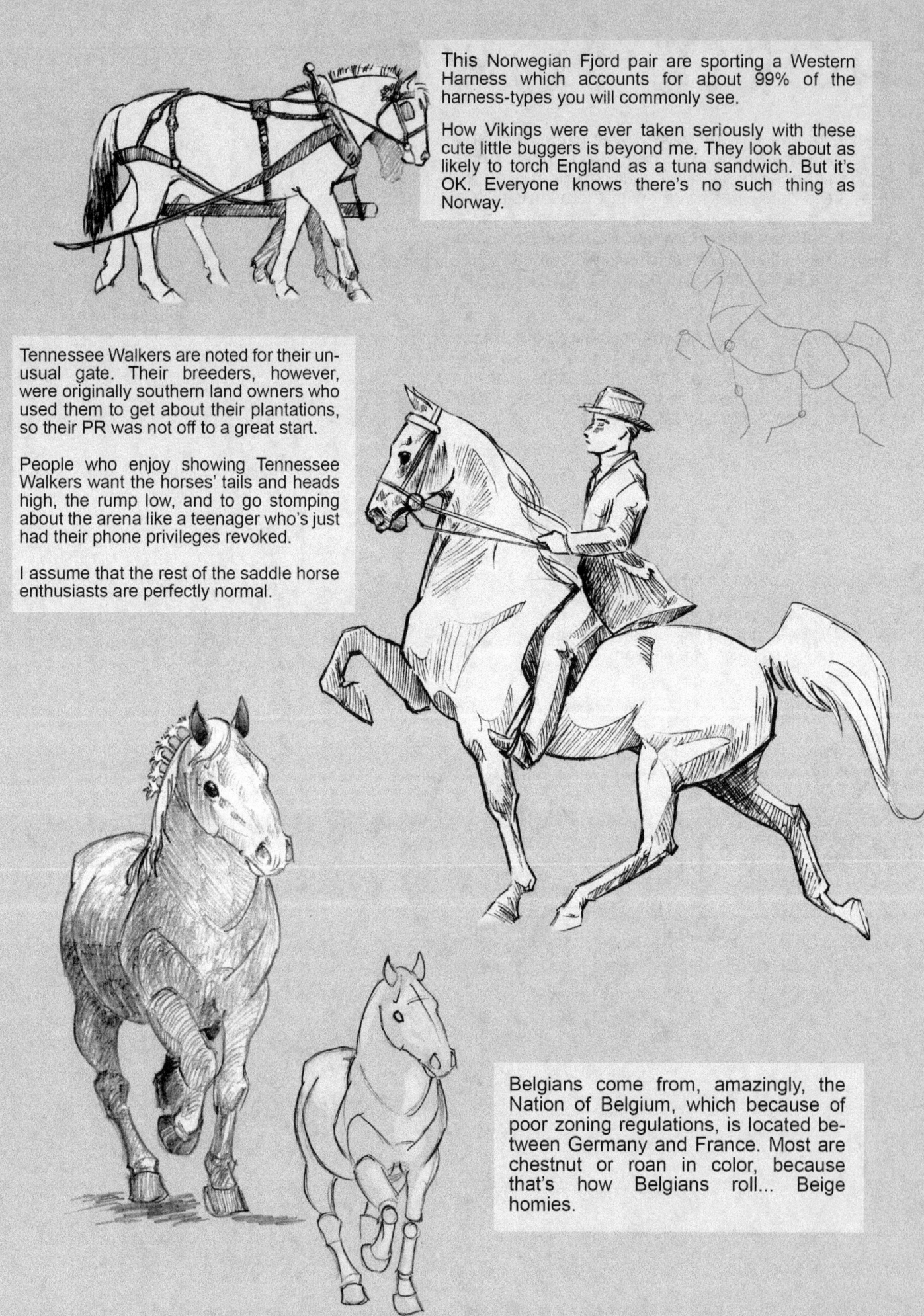

This Norwegian Fjord pair are sporting a Western Harness which accounts for about 99% of the harness-types you will commonly see.

How Vikings were ever taken seriously with these cute little buggers is beyond me. They look about as likely to torch England as a tuna sandwich. But it's OK. Everyone knows there's no such thing as Norway.

Tennessee Walkers are noted for their unusual gate. Their breeders, however, were originally southern land owners who used them to get about their plantations, so their PR was not off to a great start.

People who enjoy showing Tennessee Walkers want the horses' tails and heads high, the rump low, and to go stomping about the arena like a teenager who's just had their phone privileges revoked.

I assume that the rest of the saddle horse enthusiasts are perfectly normal.

Belgians come from, amazingly, the Nation of Belgium, which because of poor zoning regulations, is located between Germany and France. Most are chestnut or roan in color, because that's how Belgians roll... Beige homies.

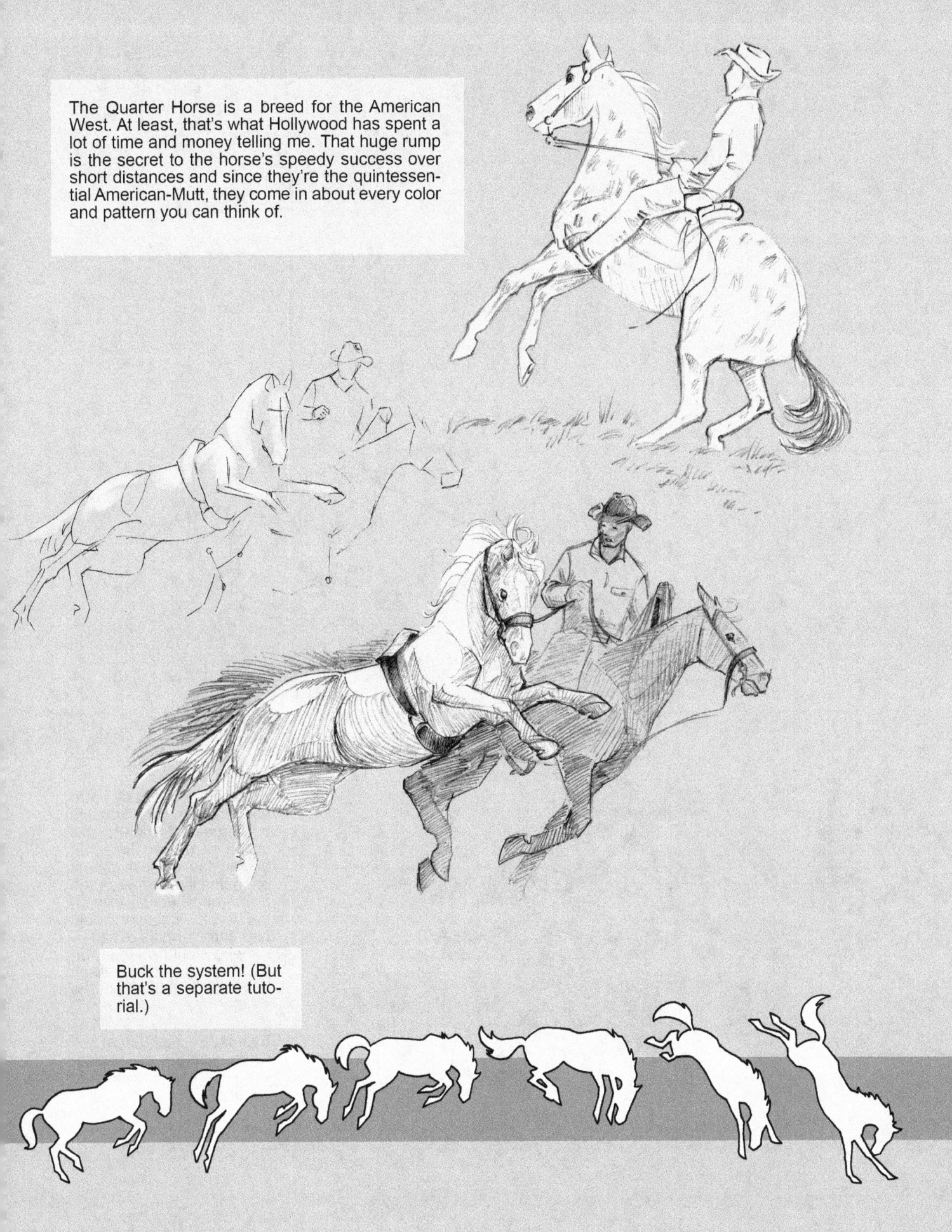

The Quarter Horse is a breed for the American West. At least, that's what Hollywood has spent a lot of time and money telling me. That huge rump is the secret to the horse's speedy success over short distances and since they're the quintessential American-Mutt, they come in about every color and pattern you can think of.

Buck the system! (But that's a separate tutorial.)

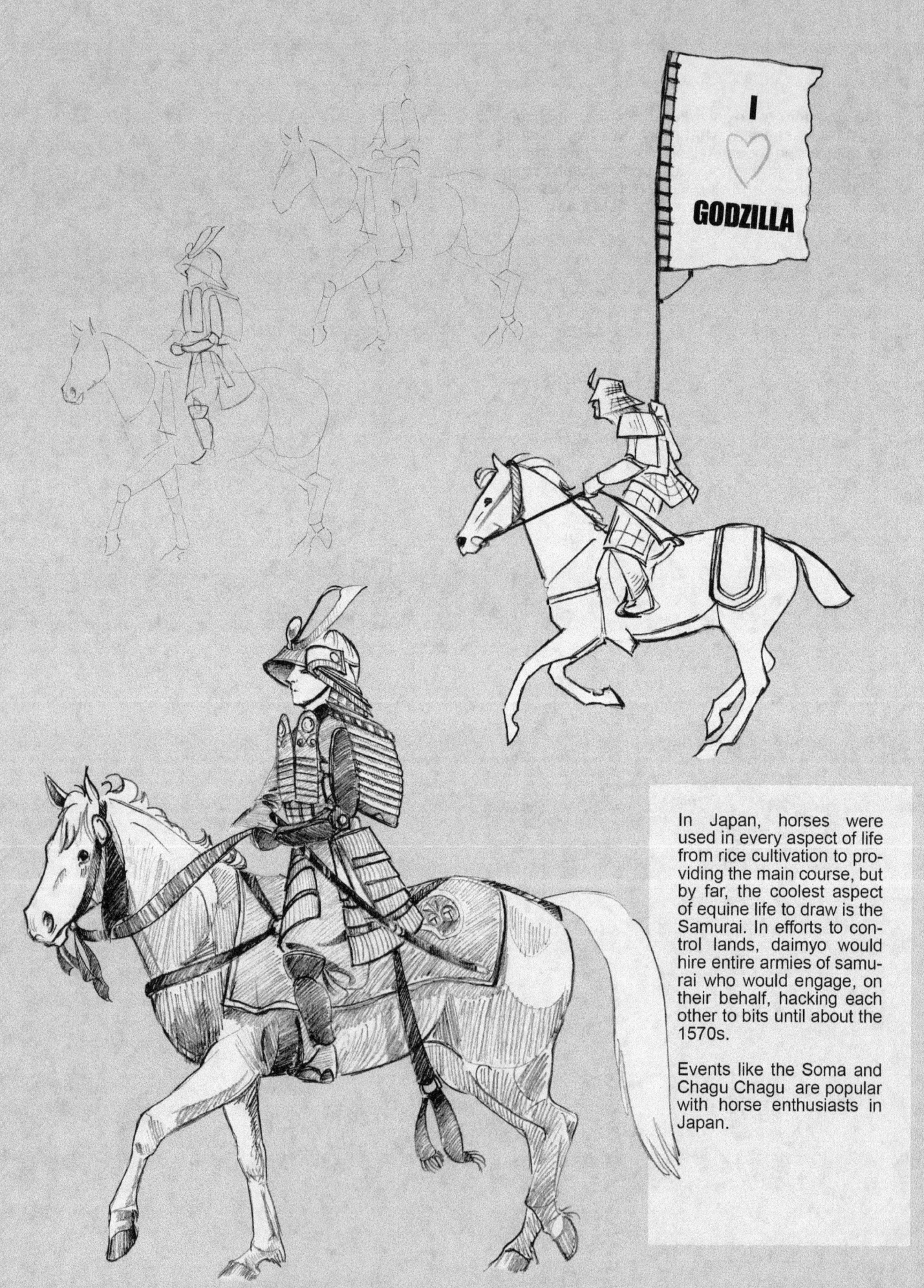

I ♥ GODZILLA

In Japan, horses were used in every aspect of life from rice cultivation to providing the main course, but by far, the coolest aspect of equine life to draw is the Samurai. In efforts to control lands, daimyo would hire entire armies of samurai who would engage, on their behalf, hacking each other to bits until about the 1570s.

Events like the Soma and Chagu Chagu are popular with horse enthusiasts in Japan.

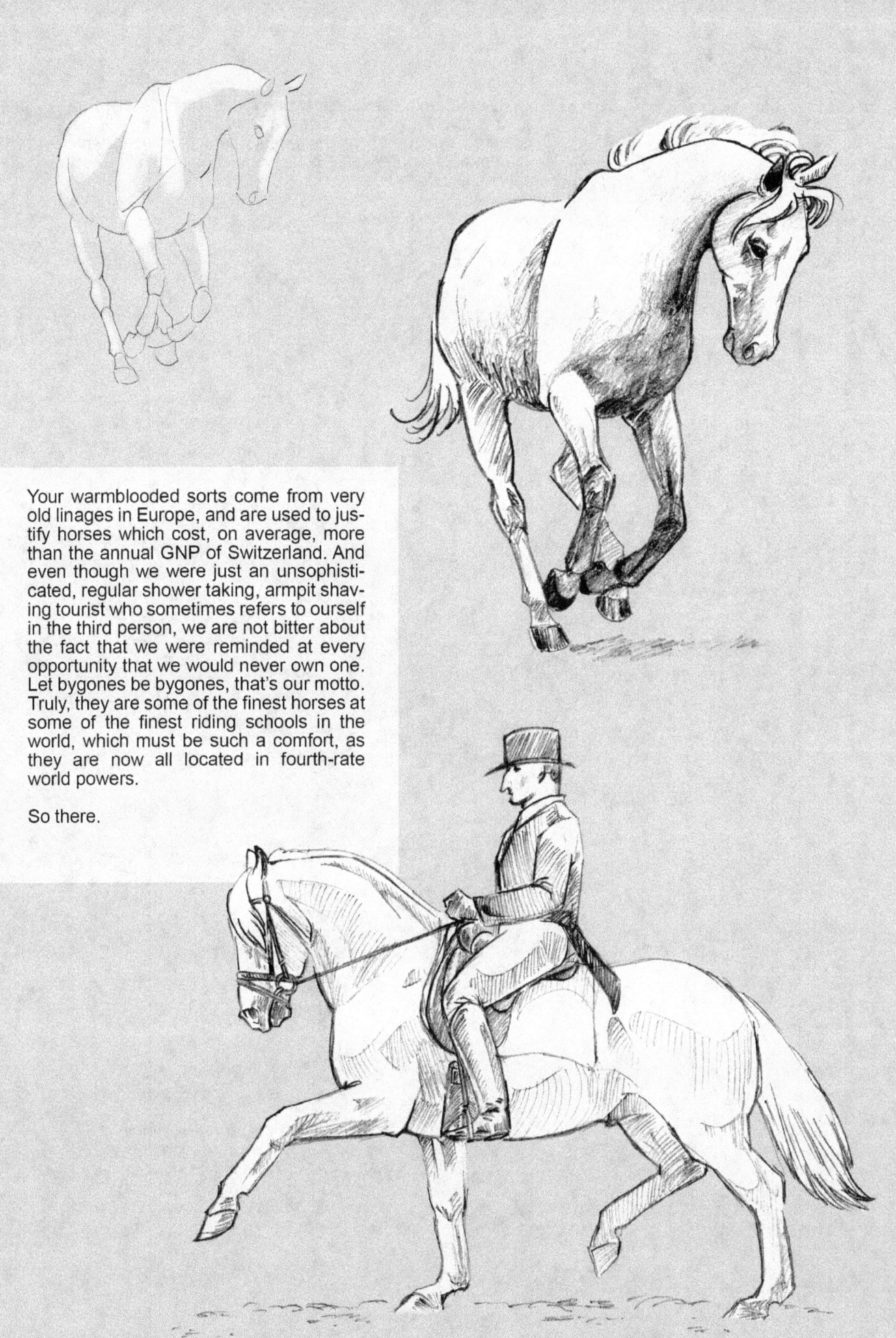

Your warmblooded sorts come from very old linages in Europe, and are used to justify horses which cost, on average, more than the annual GNP of Switzerland. And even though we were just an unsophisticated, regular shower taking, armpit shaving tourist who sometimes refers to ourself in the third person, we are not bitter about the fact that we were reminded at every opportunity that we would never own one. Let bygones be bygones, that's our motto. Truly, they are some of the finest horses at some of the finest riding schools in the world, which must be such a comfort, as they are now all located in fourth-rate world powers.

So there.

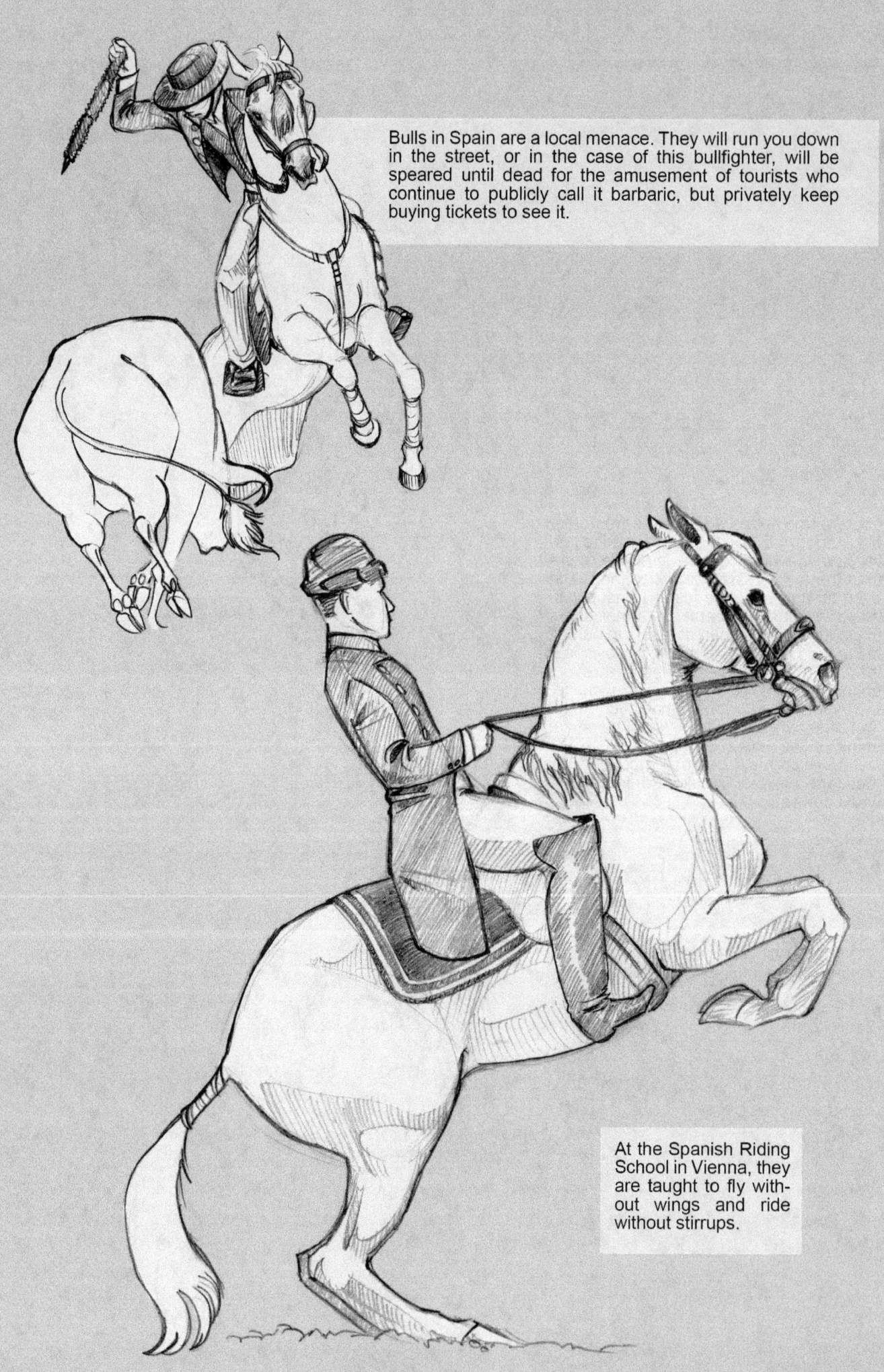

Bulls in Spain are a local menace. They will run you down in the street, or in the case of this bullfighter, will be speared until dead for the amusement of tourists who continue to publicly call it barbaric, but privately keep buying tickets to see it.

At the Spanish Riding School in Vienna, they are taught to fly without wings and ride without stirrups.

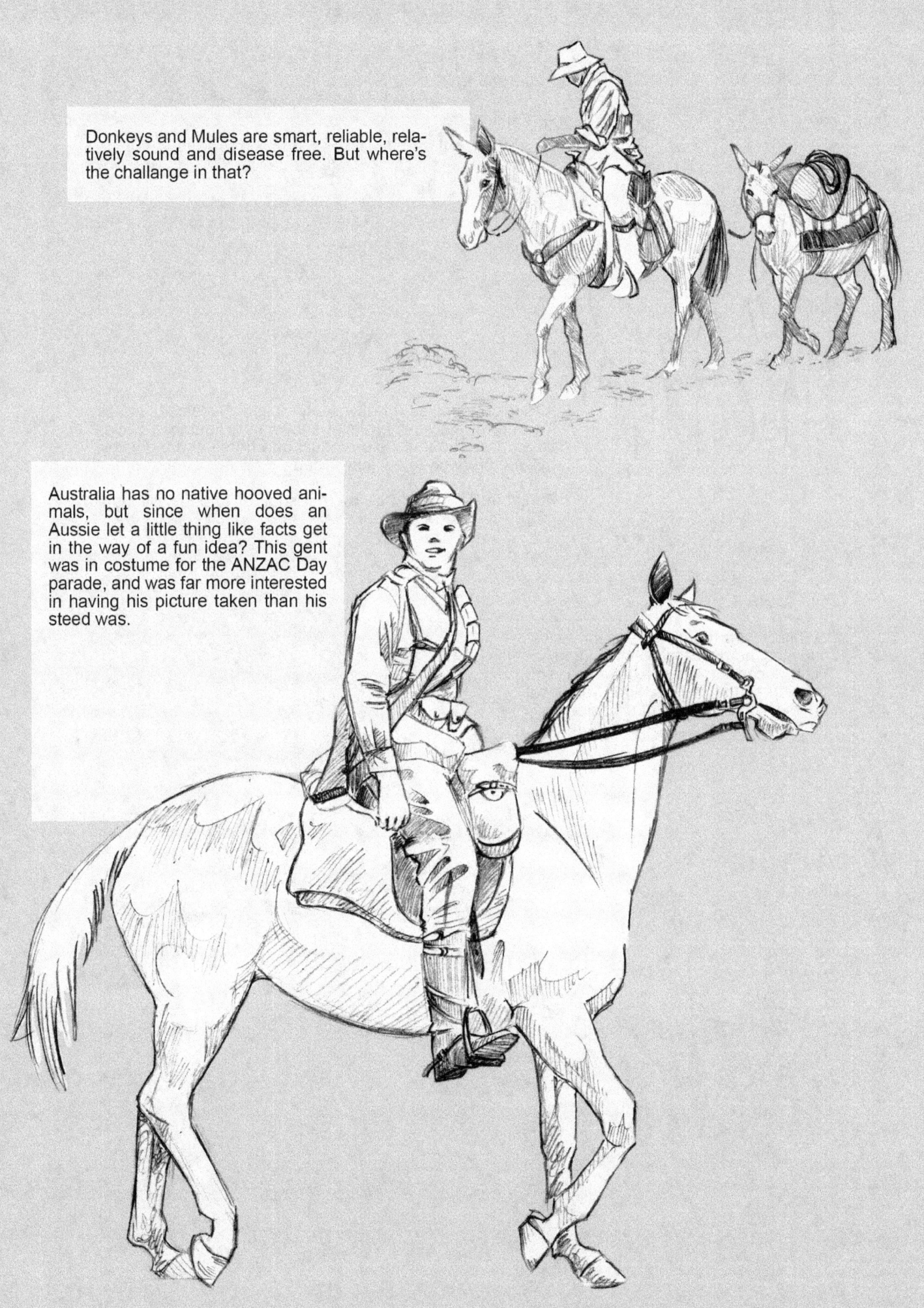

Donkeys and Mules are smart, reliable, relatively sound and disease free. But where's the challange in that?

Australia has no native hooved animals, but since when does an Aussie let a little thing like facts get in the way of a fun idea? This gent was in costume for the ANZAC Day parade, and was far more interested in having his picture taken than his steed was.

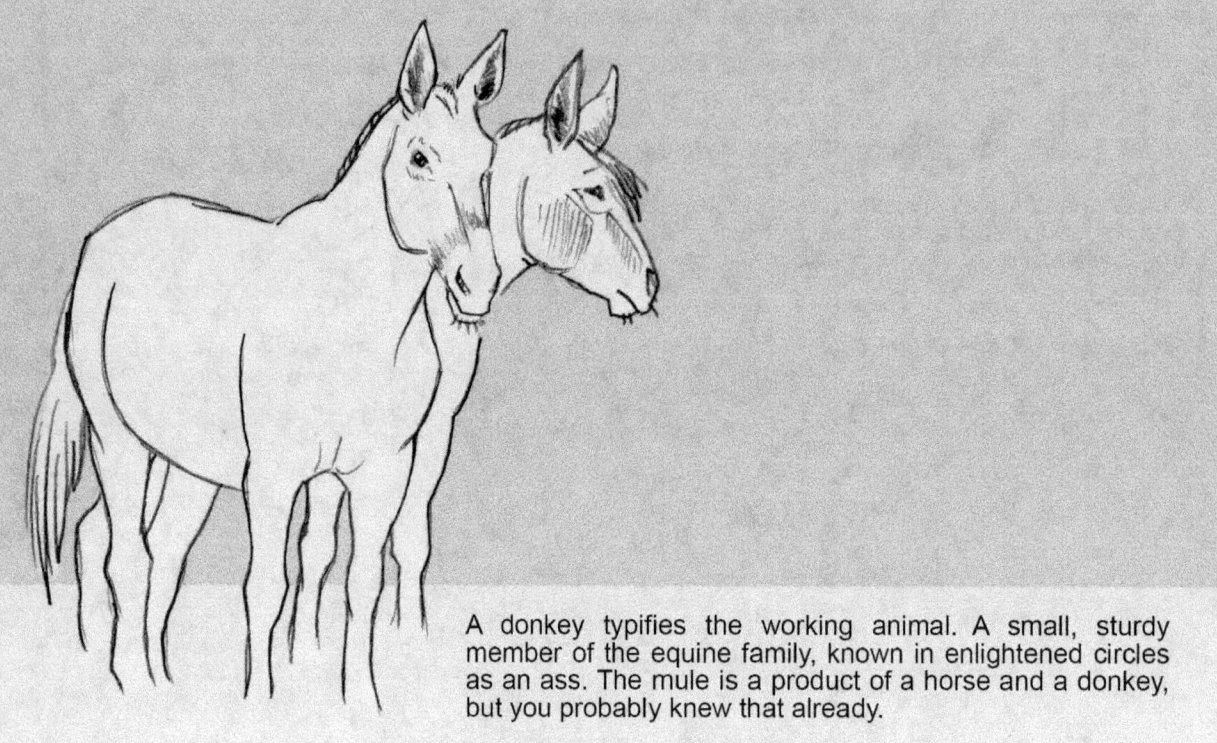

A donkey typifies the working animal. A small, sturdy member of the equine family, known in enlightened circles as an ass. The mule is a product of a horse and a donkey, but you probably knew that already.

Footnote: This would be a great spot for a terrifically inappropriate jackass reference.

While roving bands of unsubmissive, spirited herds captivate the imagination, I can say from experience, you only need to travel as far as your local horse classifieds to meet some truly untamed animals.

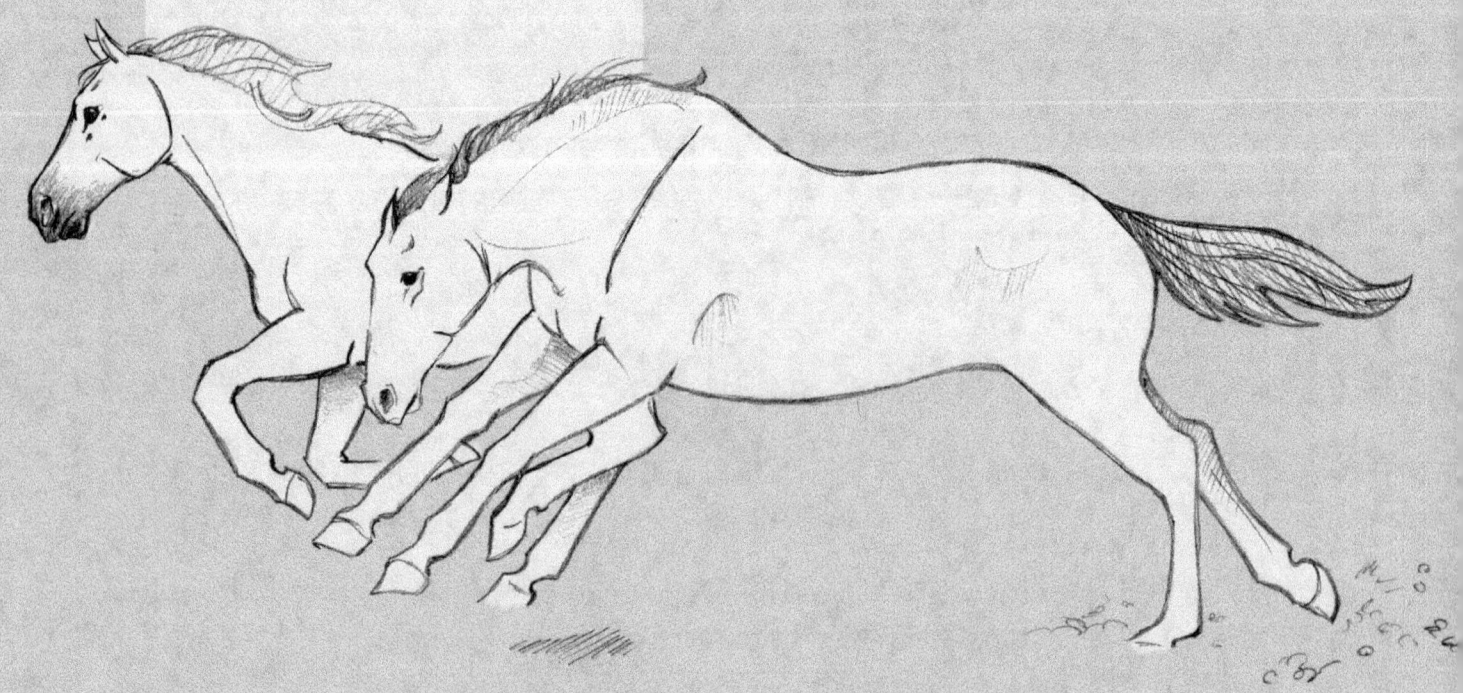

The Shire is a breed from Ye Olde United Kingdom which is popular as a country for speaking some English. Shires were bred as work horses and so that the English could say, "Neener Neener, my horse is bigger than yours!" To which the French would point out that they had an outrageous accent, *and* sauce, which is what led to the battle of Agincourt.

(Actually, despite my best efforts, historians continue to point out the fact that the shire was not actually used in any medieval warfare because, if you want to get technical about it, the breed didn't exist yet. Your average warhorse then stood around 15 hands, which is just a shame, because Shires look wicked-cool playing the part.)

Historians can be inconsiderate like that.

While knightly armor was all about defense, sometimes looking a bit flash would get you by. This knight is geared up for looks, not the battlefield.

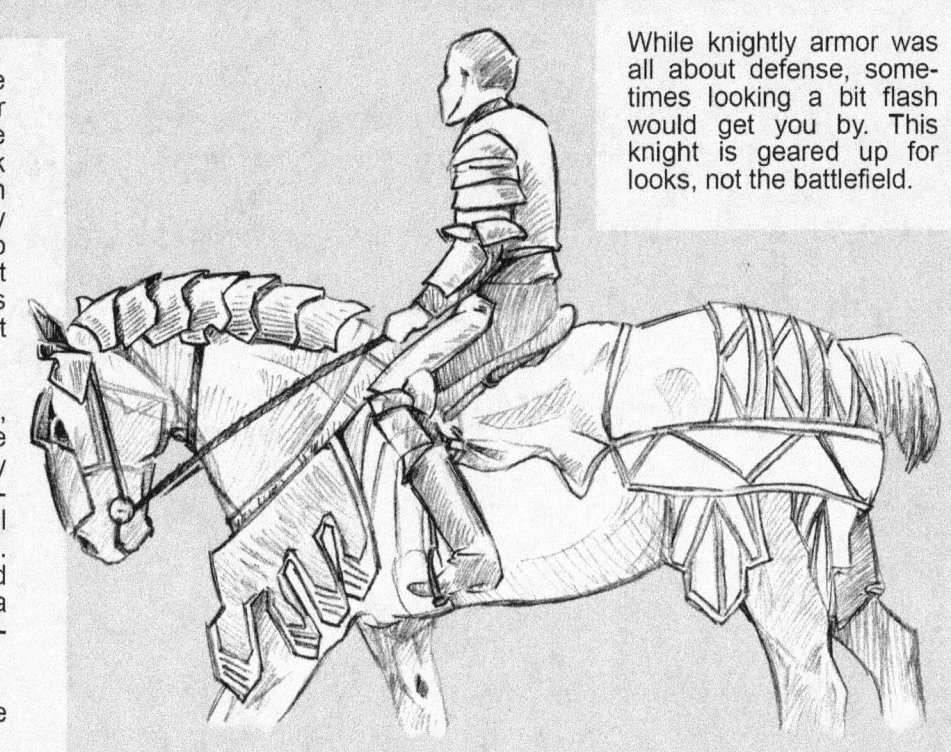

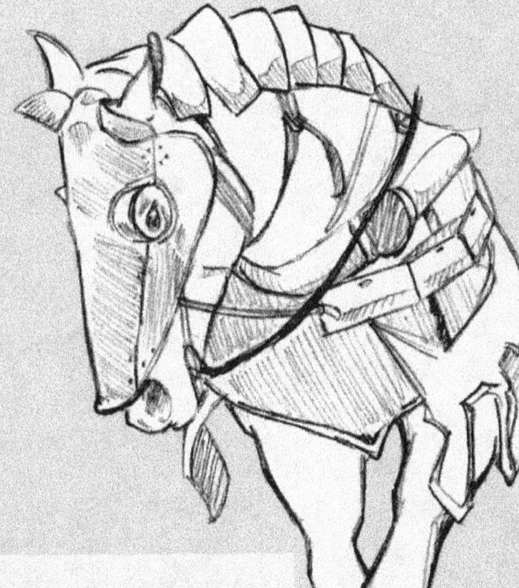

Knight's costume from the front.

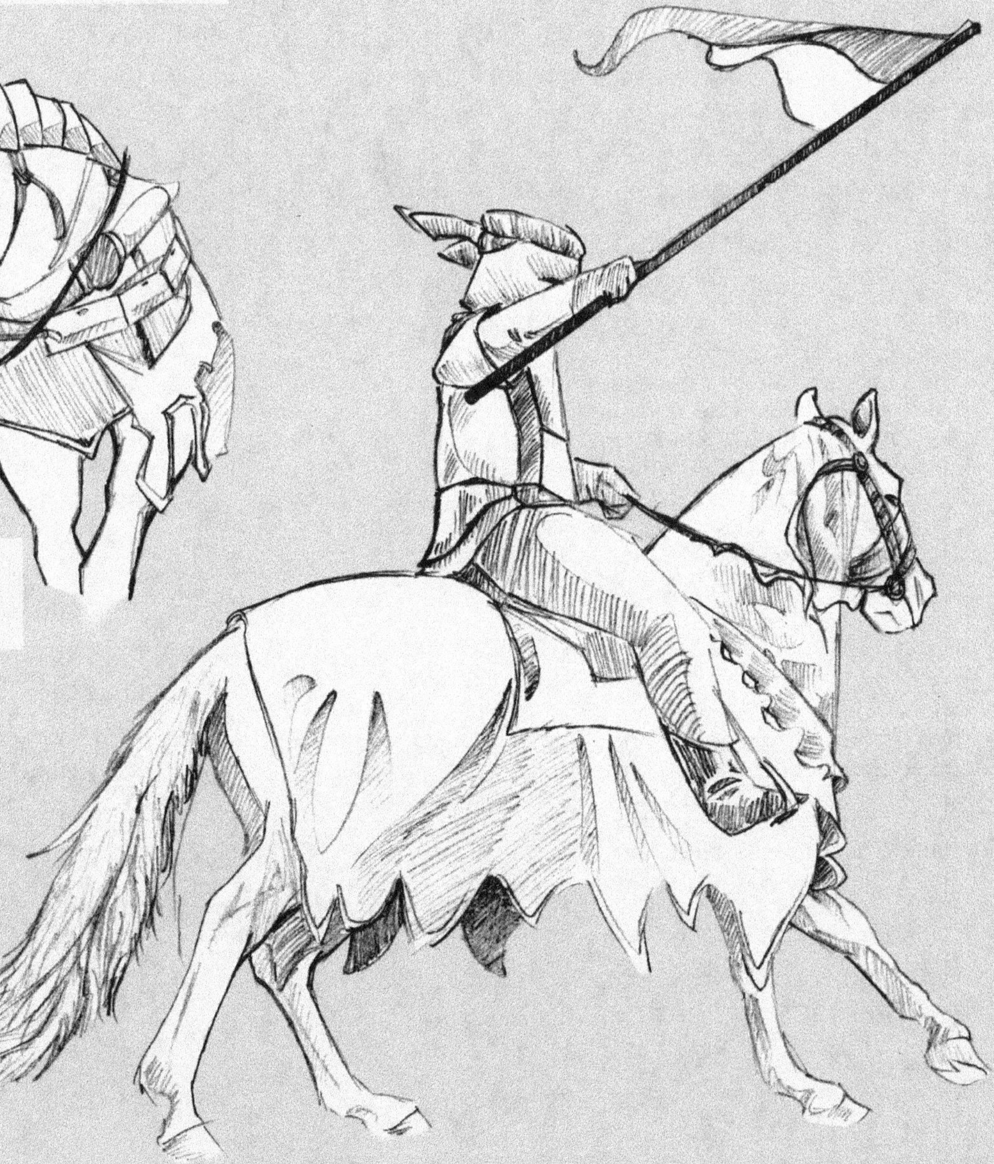

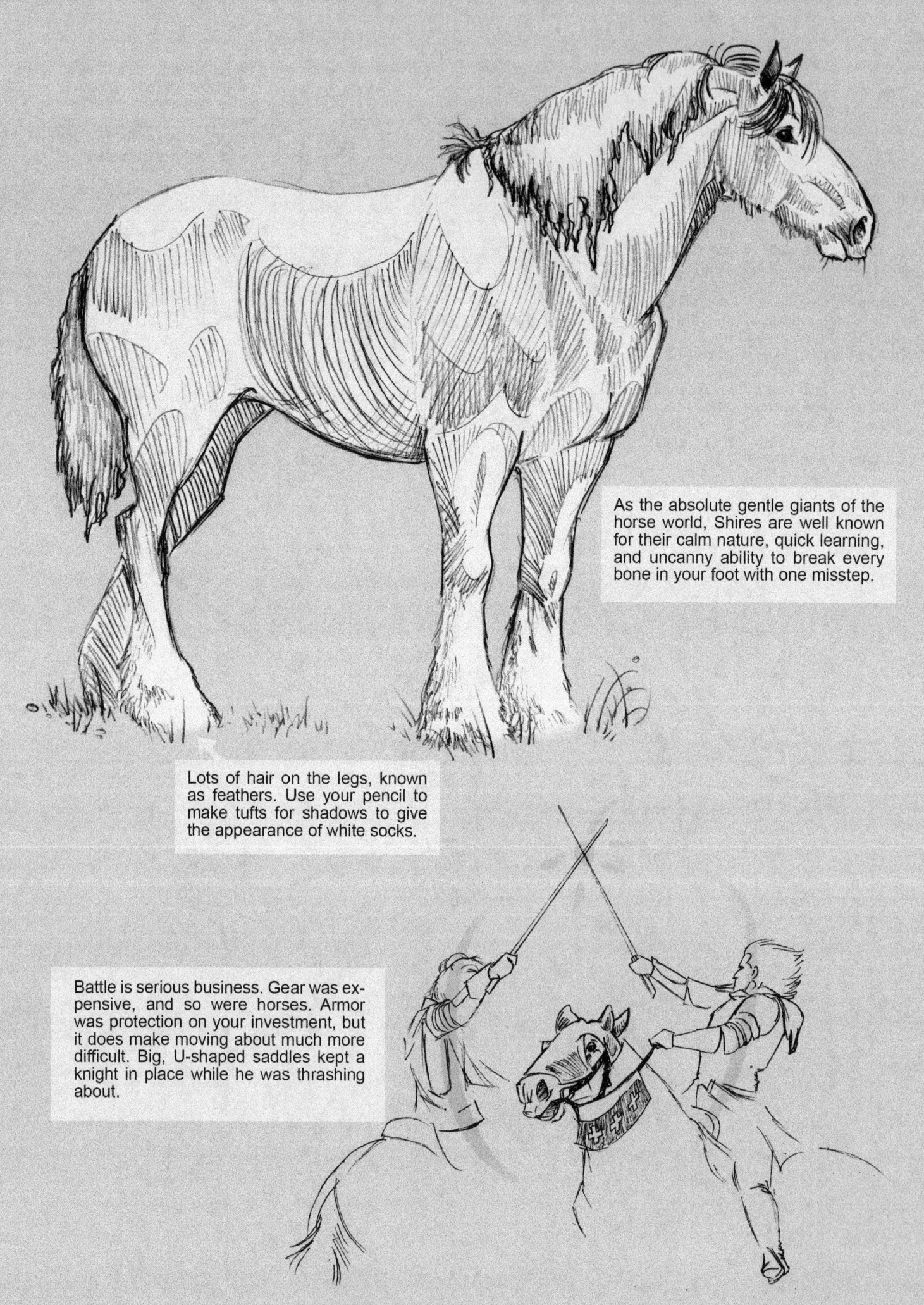

As the absolute gentle giants of the horse world, Shires are well known for their calm nature, quick learning, and uncanny ability to break every bone in your foot with one misstep.

Lots of hair on the legs, known as feathers. Use your pencil to make tufts for shadows to give the appearance of white socks.

Battle is serious business. Gear was expensive, and so were horses. Armor was protection on your investment, but it does make moving about much more difficult. Big, U-shaped saddles kept a knight in place while he was thrashing about.

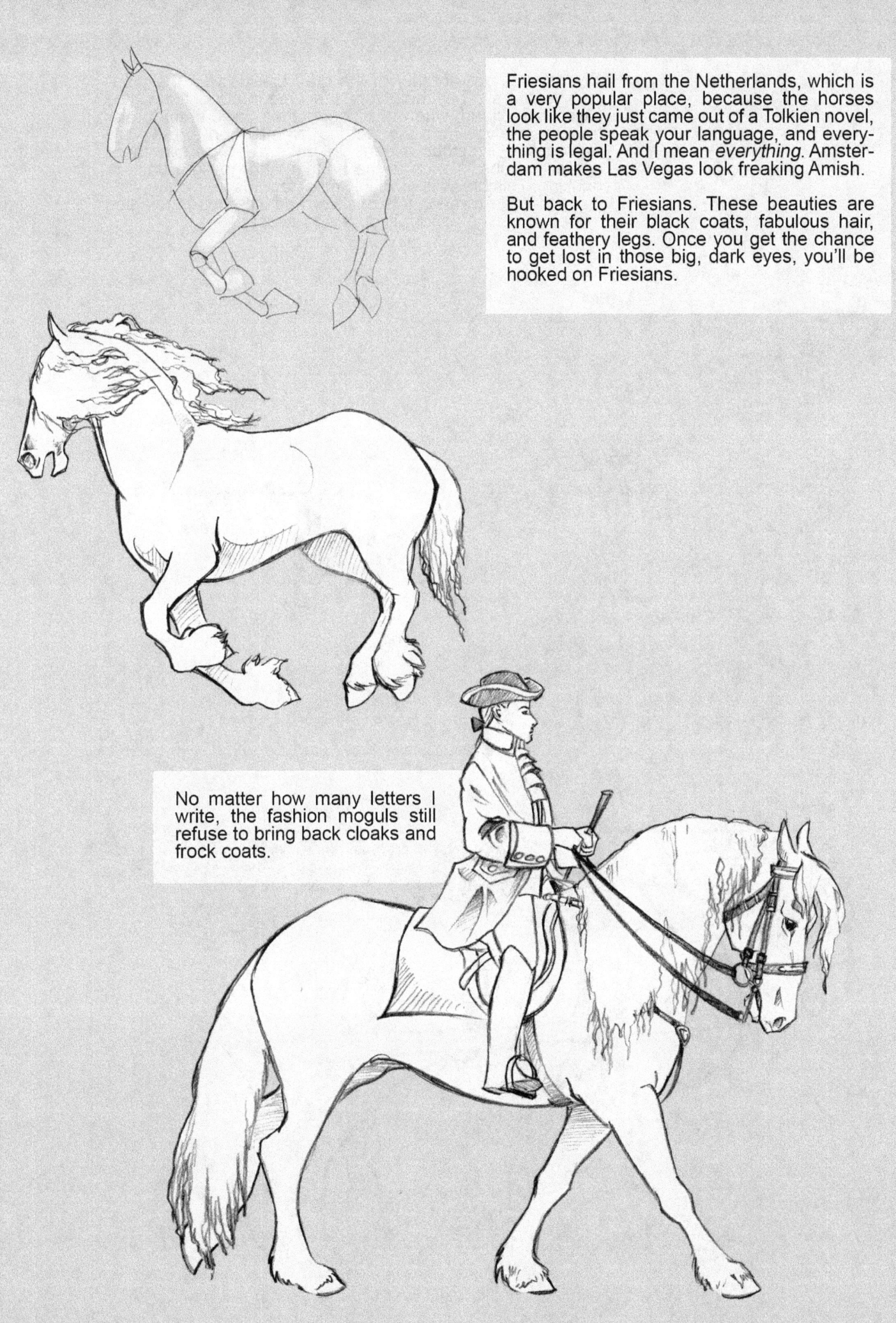

Friesians hail from the Netherlands, which is a very popular place, because the horses look like they just came out of a Tolkien novel, the people speak your language, and everything is legal. And I mean *everything*. Amsterdam makes Las Vegas look freaking Amish.

But back to Friesians. These beauties are known for their black coats, fabulous hair, and feathery legs. Once you get the chance to get lost in those big, dark eyes, you'll be hooked on Friesians.

No matter how many letters I write, the fashion moguls still refuse to bring back cloaks and frock coats.

Clydesdales are another of the draft breeds with the fabulous feathers. They hail from the area around the Clyde River in Scotland, where the people there bred them to distract themselves from the fact that all they had to eat were overcooked livestock organs in pubs. The people there gather in pubs, glance at the haggis, and go right back to drinking. This breed is probably most famous for pulling beer wagons while wearing lots of silver and little ribbon thingies in their mane. (Alcohol will do this to people.)

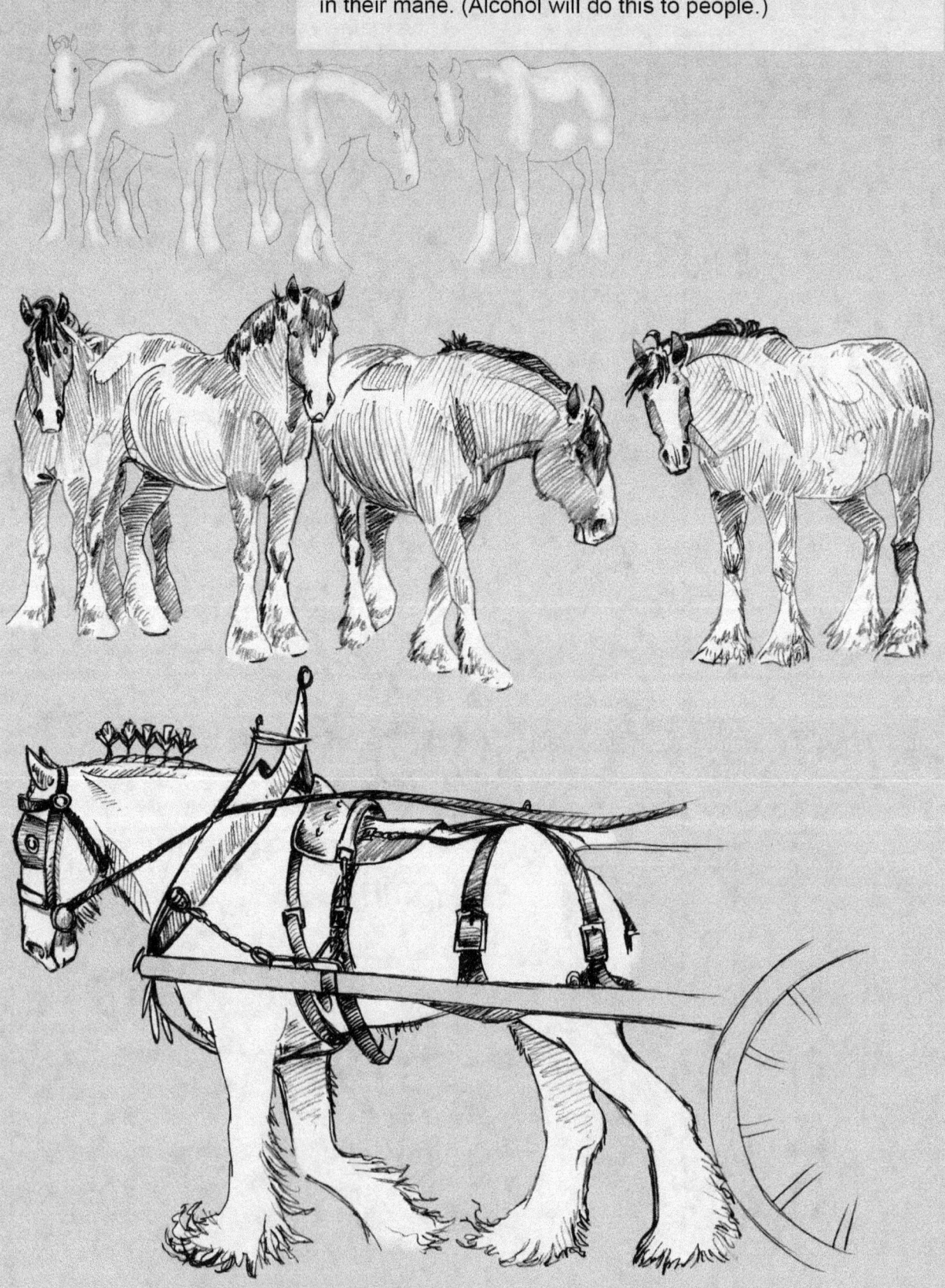

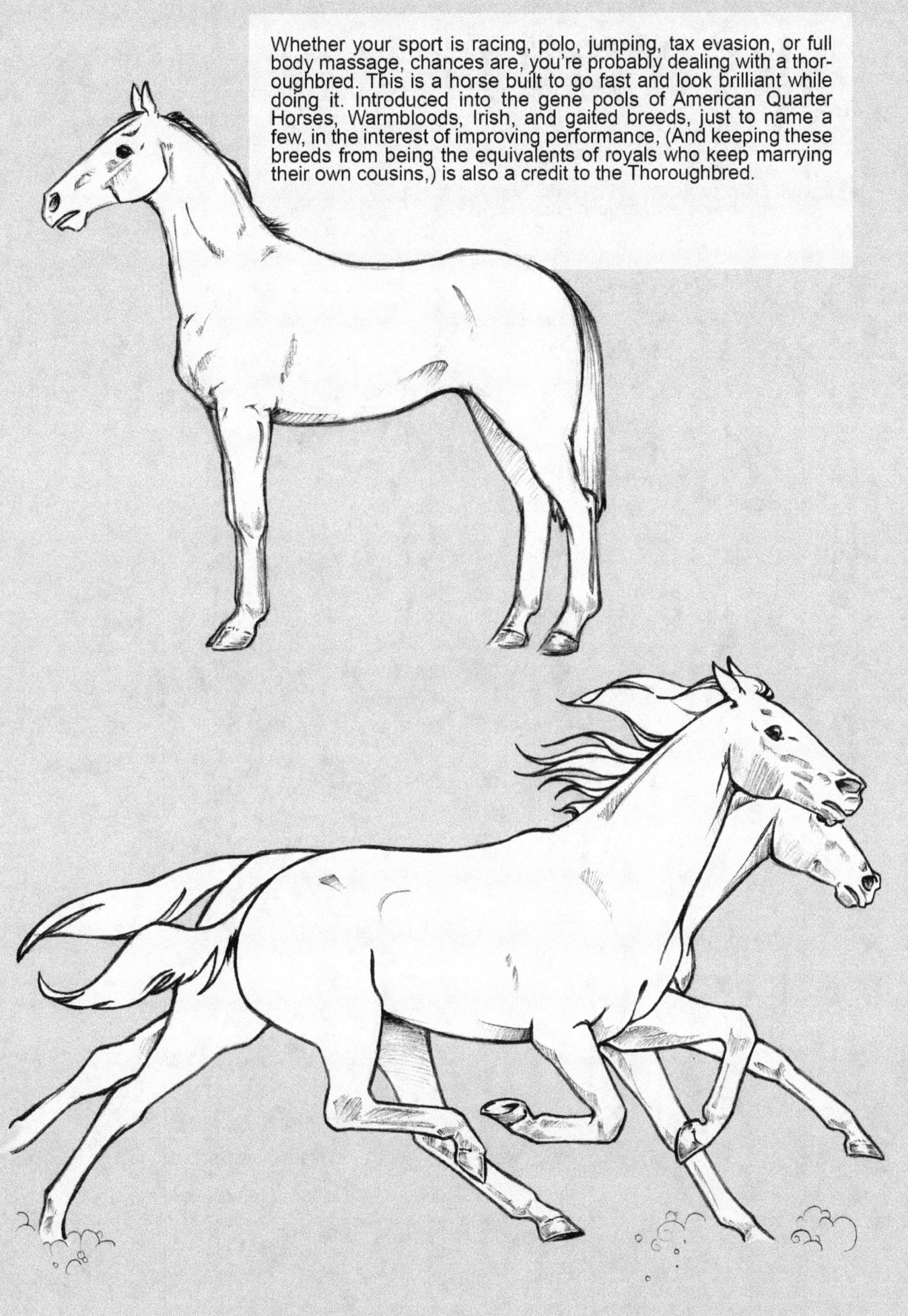

Whether your sport is racing, polo, jumping, tax evasion, or full body massage, chances are, you're probably dealing with a thoroughbred. This is a horse built to go fast and look brilliant while doing it. Introduced into the gene pools of American Quarter Horses, Warmbloods, Irish, and gaited breeds, just to name a few, in the interest of improving performance, (And keeping these breeds from being the equivalents of royals who keep marrying their own cousins,) is also a credit to the Thoroughbred.

AH, YOUTH

When it comes to character acting, babies steal the show. Overly long legs, gangly coordination, fluffy mane and tail... they're so cute, it makes me wonder what they're really up to.

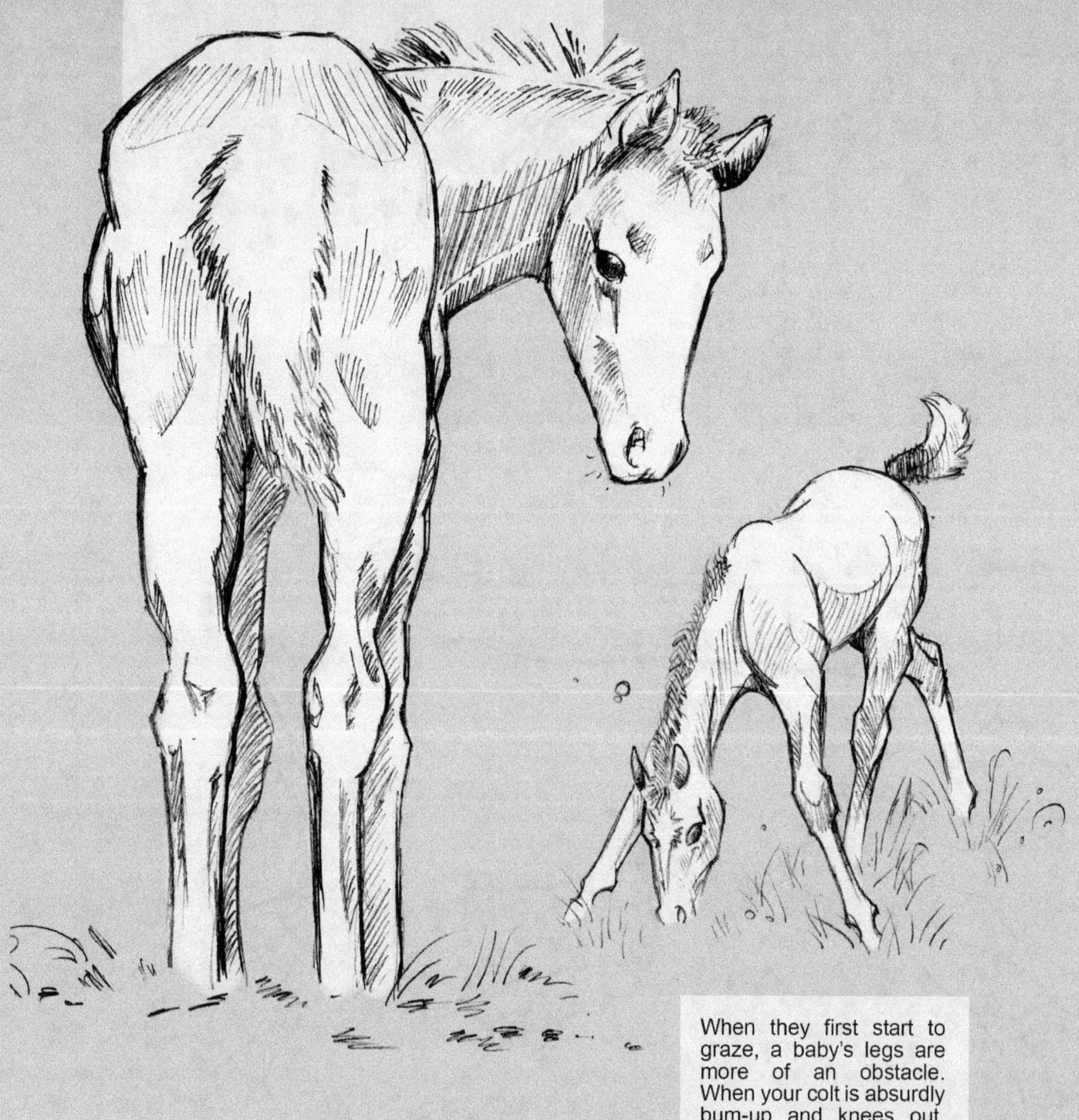

When they first start to graze, a baby's legs are more of an obstacle. When your colt is absurdly bum-up and knees out, you're drawing him right.

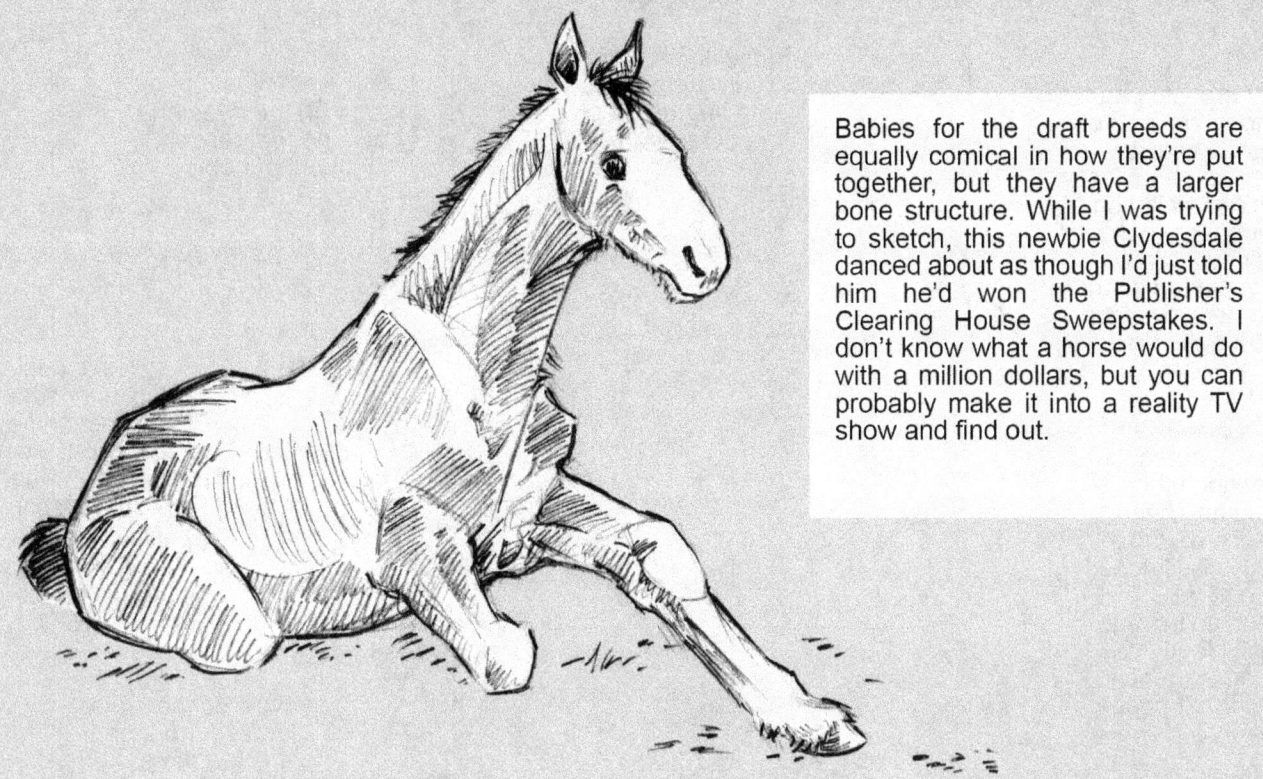

Babies for the draft breeds are equally comical in how they're put together, but they have a larger bone structure. While I was trying to sketch, this newbie Clydesdale danced about as though I'd just told him he'd won the Publisher's Clearing House Sweepstakes. I don't know what a horse would do with a million dollars, but you can probably make it into a reality TV show and find out.

Mares, you will discover, are remarkably liberal about feeding in public.

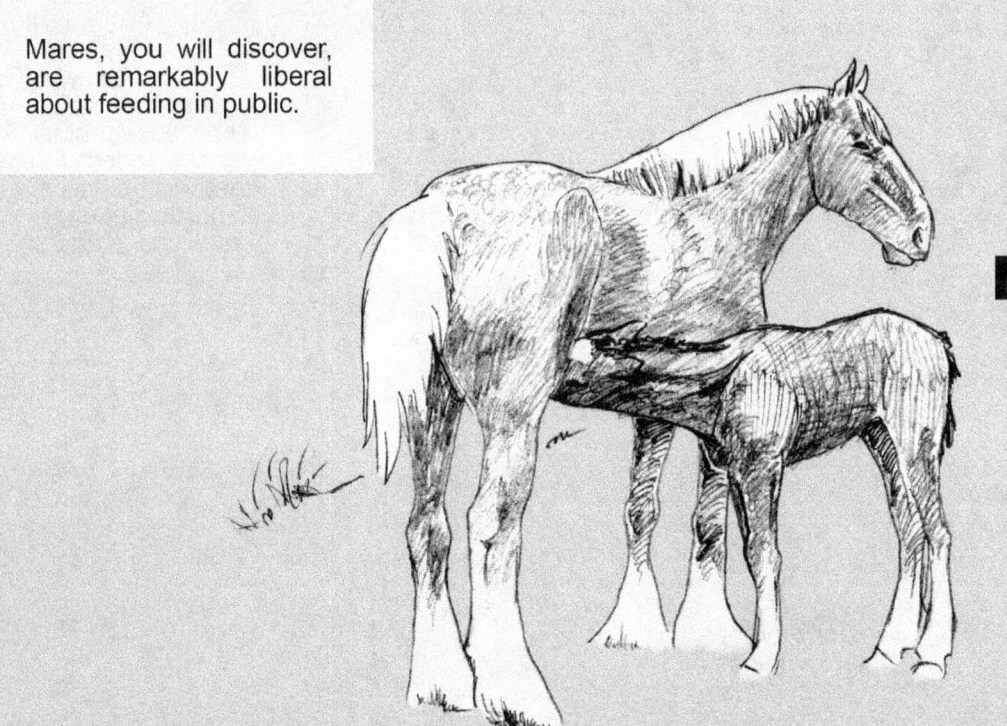

NOM NOM NOM

REN FAIR REAR

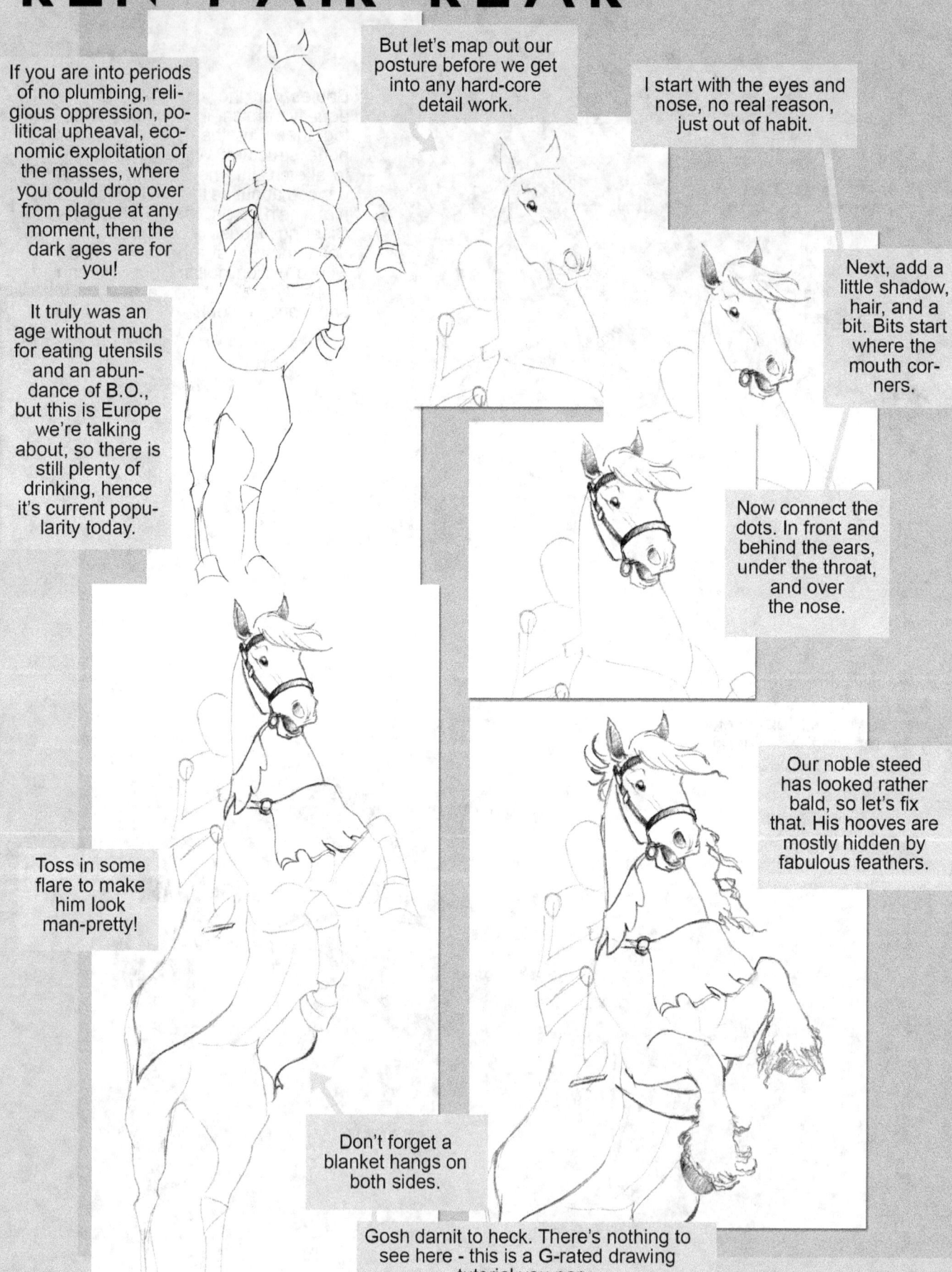

If you are into periods of no plumbing, religious oppression, political upheaval, economic exploitation of the masses, where you could drop over from plague at any moment, then the dark ages are for you!

It truly was an age without much for eating utensils and an abundance of B.O., but this is Europe we're talking about, so there is still plenty of drinking, hence it's current popularity today.

But let's map out our posture before we get into any hard-core detail work.

I start with the eyes and nose, no real reason, just out of habit.

Next, add a little shadow, hair, and a bit. Bits start where the mouth corners.

Now connect the dots. In front and behind the ears, under the throat, and over the nose.

Our noble steed has looked rather bald, so let's fix that. His hooves are mostly hidden by fabulous feathers.

Toss in some flare to make him look man-pretty!

Don't forget a blanket hangs on both sides.

Gosh darnit to heck. There's nothing to see here - this is a G-rated drawing tutorial you perv.

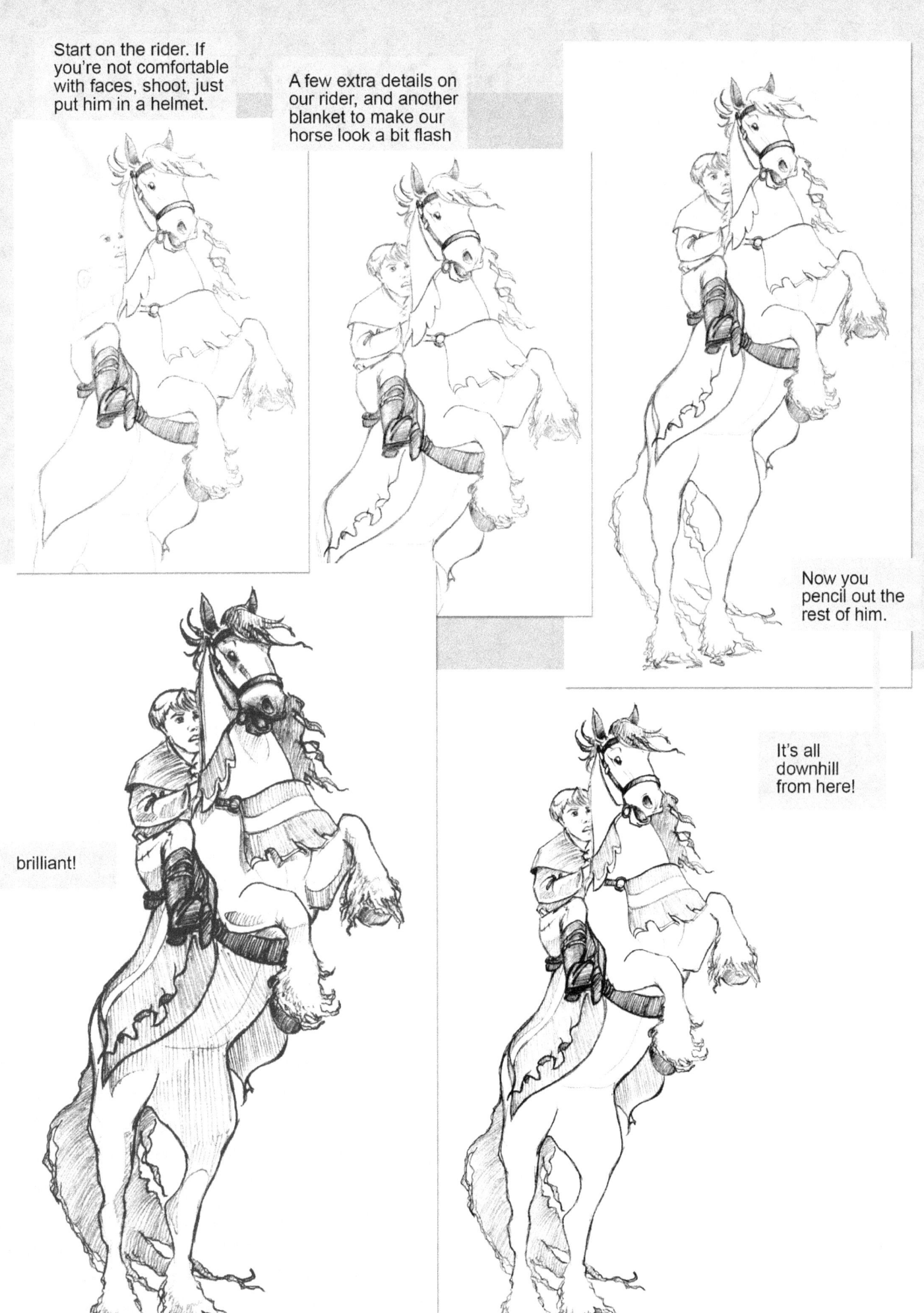

Start on the rider. If you're not comfortable with faces, shoot, just put him in a helmet.

A few extra details on our rider, and another blanket to make our horse look a bit flash

Now you pencil out the rest of him.

brilliant!

It's all downhill from here!

PLOWIN' NOW TEAM

Every year in July, the town of Taylor in North Dakota explodes with horses and the finest collection of 1920s farming equipment you have ever seen. There are performing actors, blacksmiths, sorted demonstrations, and with permission, you can get real close and pet the animals. Sometimes, they'll let you pet the horses too.

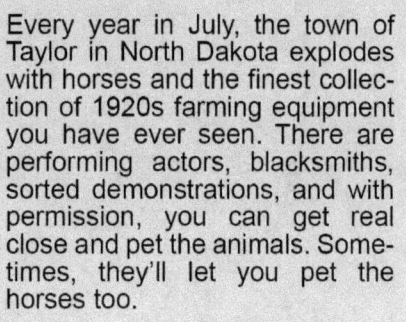

So to start with, shapes are our friends. I've also sketched a horizon line, so we have a guess where the ground ends and the sky begins.

Then you add another horse to the team. Most of the second teamster will be covered by the first, but since he's further away, he should look just a tish smaller.

Last bit here - wheels go on either side of our plow, and everything else fits inbetween. Our guy sits in the middle, (He must have a nice view, huh?), and I've gone and covered up half his head with a hat.

OK, so we have a good framework. Time to build up.

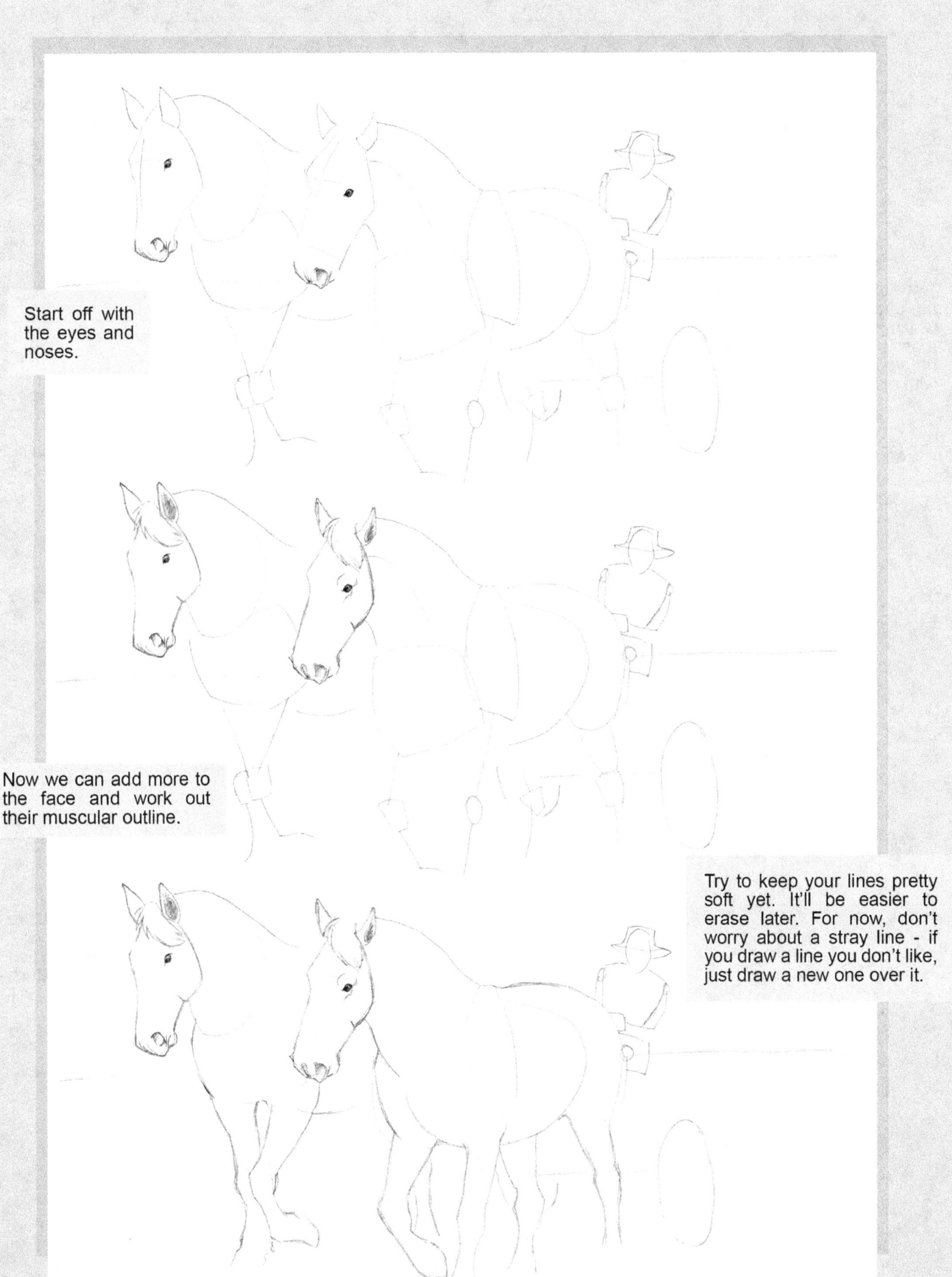

Start off with
the eyes and
noses.

Now we can add more to
the face and work out
their muscular outline.

Try to keep your lines pretty
soft yet. It'll be easier to
erase later. For now, don't
worry about a stray line - if
you draw a line you don't like,
just draw a new one over it.

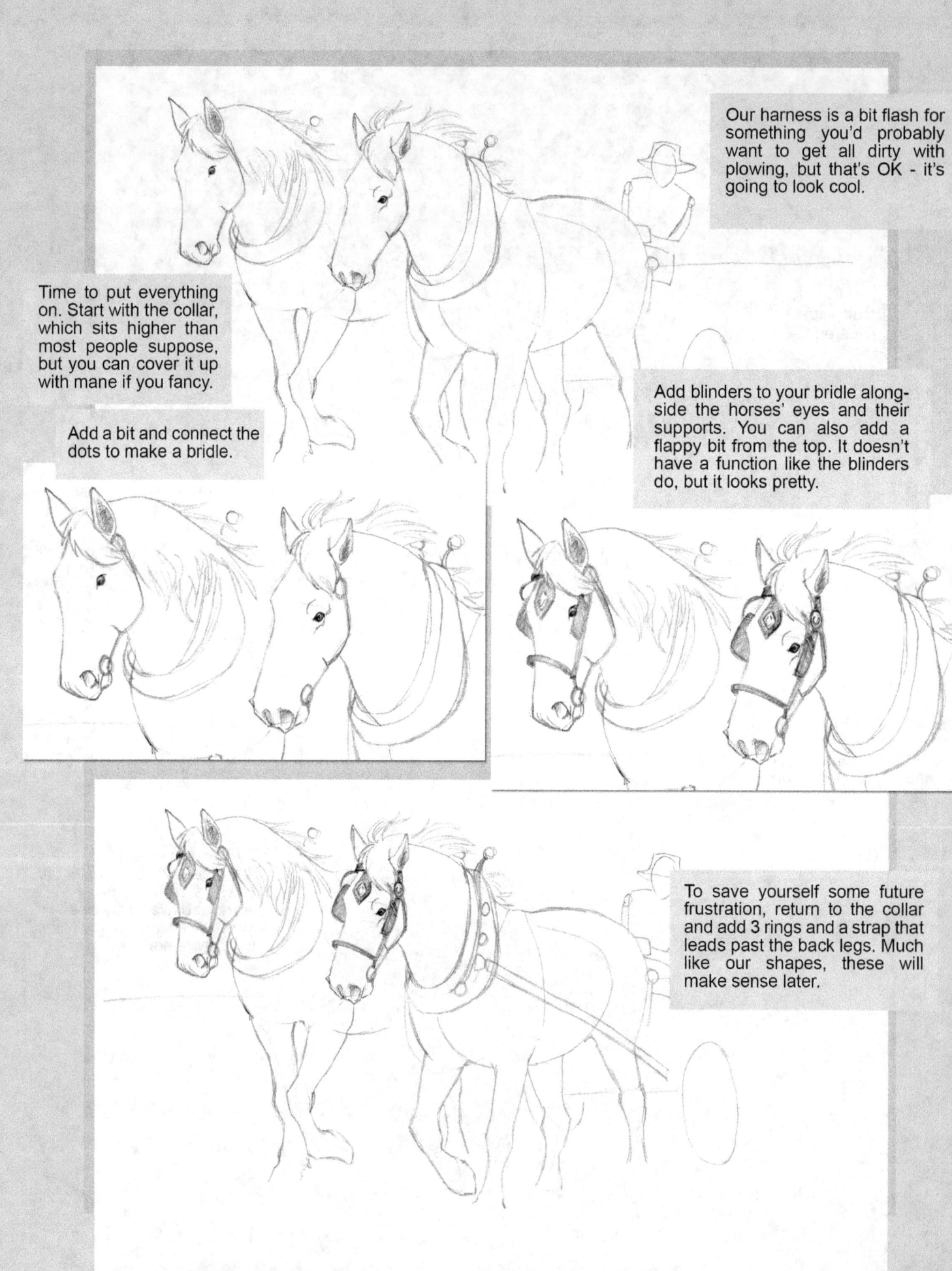

Our harness is a bit flash for something you'd probably want to get all dirty with plowing, but that's OK - it's going to look cool.

Time to put everything on. Start with the collar, which sits higher than most people suppose, but you can cover it up with mane if you fancy.

Add a bit and connect the dots to make a bridle.

Add blinders to your bridle alongside the horses' eyes and their supports. You can also add a flappy bit from the top. It doesn't have a function like the blinders do, but it looks pretty.

To save yourself some future frustration, return to the collar and add 3 rings and a strap that leads past the back legs. Much like our shapes, these will make sense later.

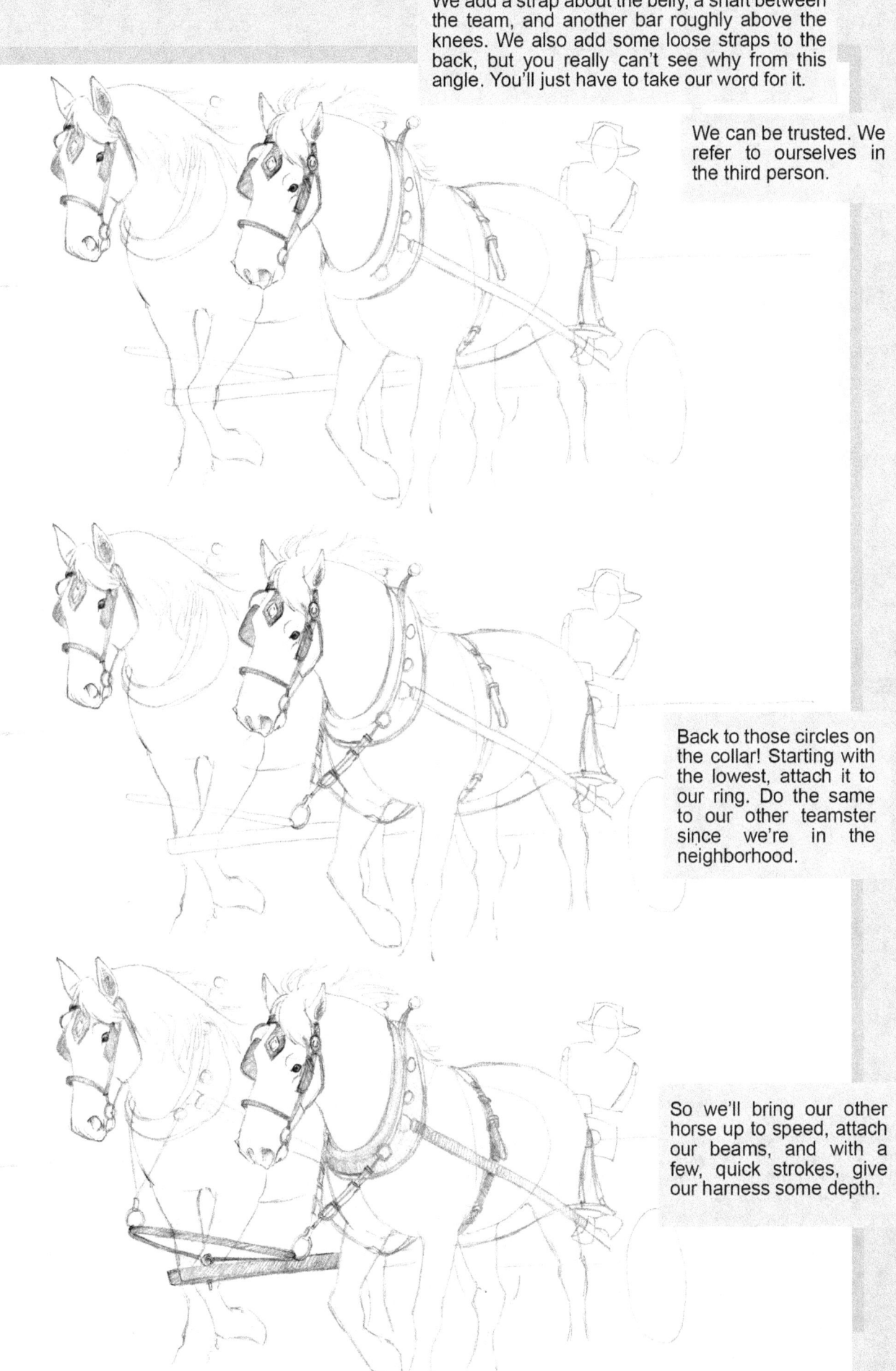

We add a strap about the belly, a shaft between the team, and another bar roughly above the knees. We also add some loose straps to the back, but you really can't see why from this angle. You'll just have to take our word for it.

We can be trusted. We refer to ourselves in the third person.

Back to those circles on the collar! Starting with the lowest, attach it to our ring. Do the same to our other teamster since we're in the neighborhood.

So we'll bring our other horse up to speed, attach our beams, and with a few, quick strokes, give our harness some depth.

Our hero's gaze puts his hat nearly level to his eyes, and since the suspension of this ride would probably reduce his spine into chicken tika, his posture is relaxed, shoulders forward, and leaning.

Draw a loose 'X' between our team, and circle where they cross with another ring.

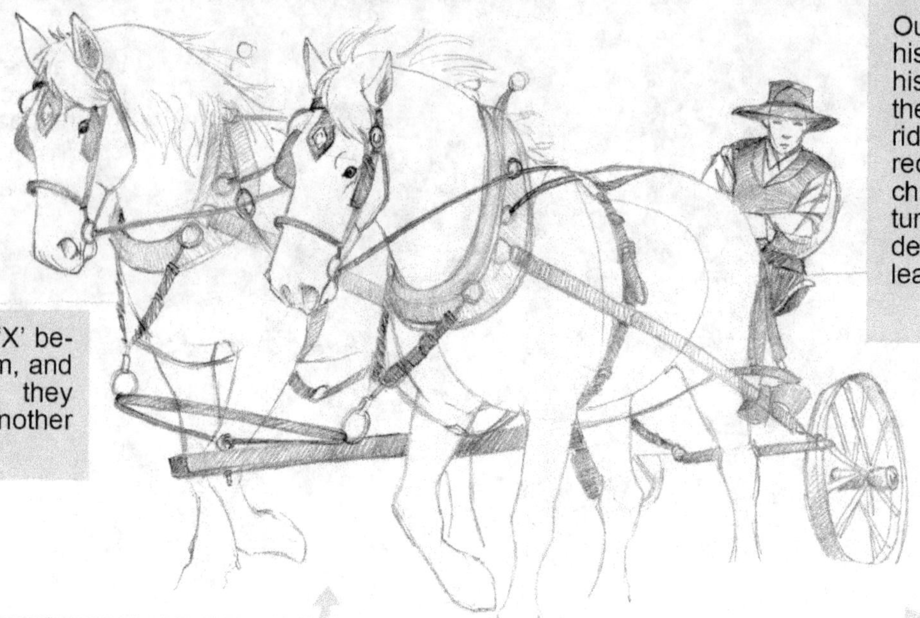

Power steering! The reign connects from the bit through the top ring on our collar. Hook another line from the second ring over the top of his back too.

Add some wheels to this operation. Don't fret about them being perfectly round or straight - farm machinery has a rough lifestyle and is always nicked up.

Don't sweat it about the plow, this is a horse drawing tutorial. A few shapely shadows towards the back gives the impression of equipment we're going for.

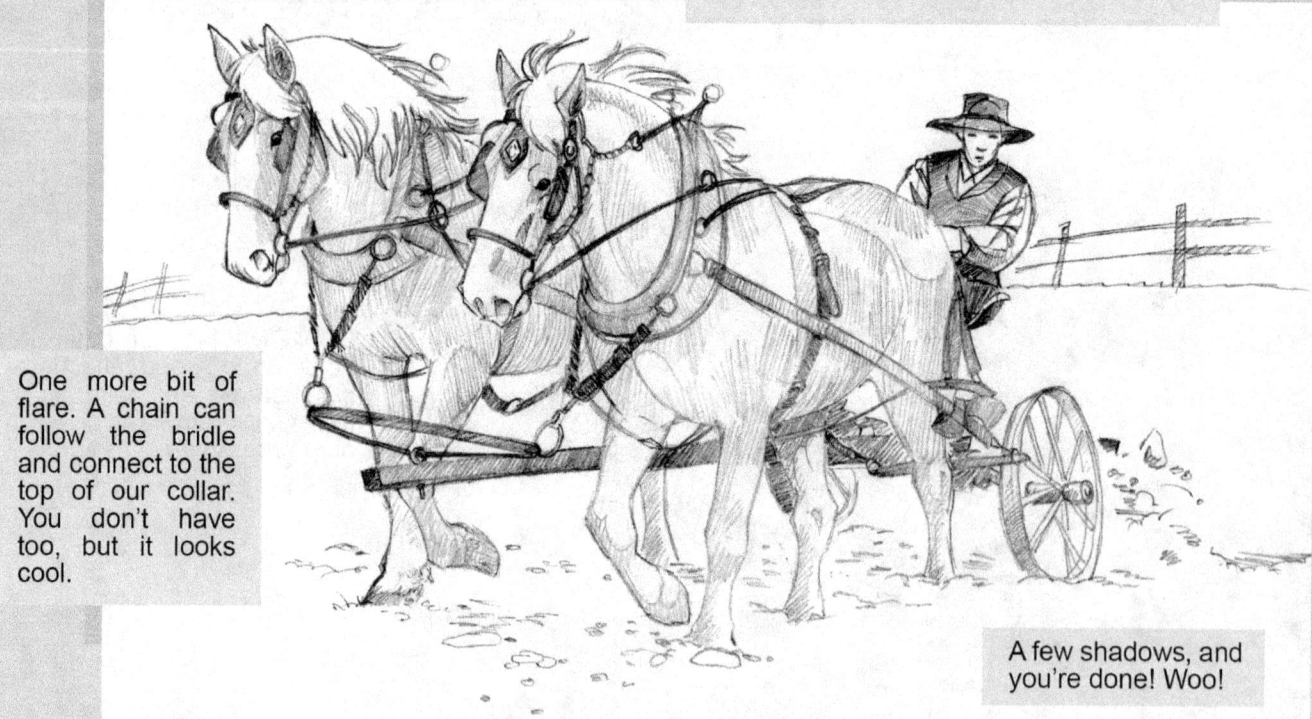

One more bit of flare. A chain can follow the bridle and connect to the top of our collar. You don't have too, but it looks cool.

A few shadows, and you're done! Woo!

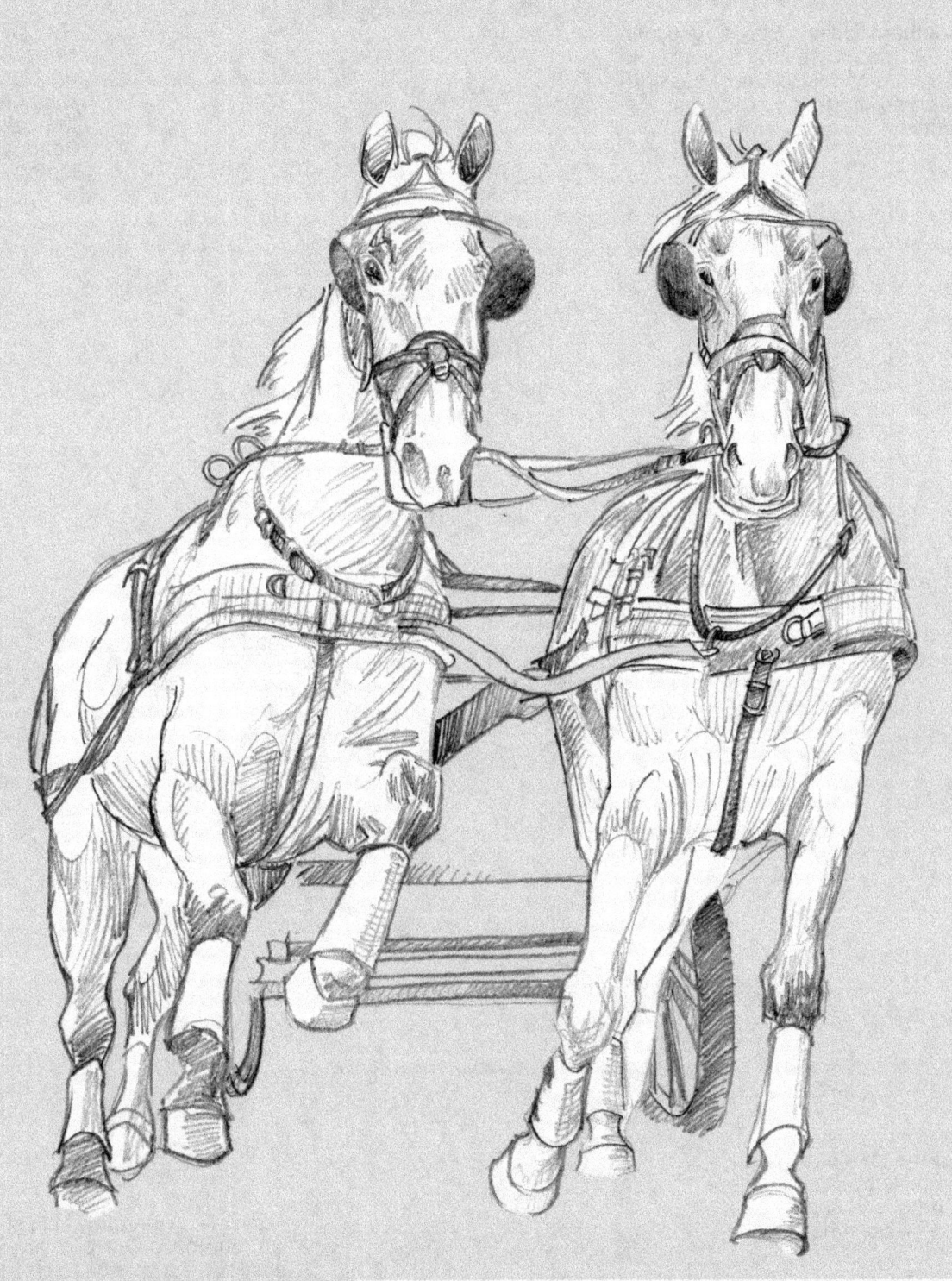

While there are different styles of bridles and harnesses out there, over time and across disciplines, things haven't really changed too much over all. There are only so many ways to effectively put straps and rings together on a horse. This racing harness from today works on the same principles as ancient chariots.

CIVIL WAR STEED

In the southern United States, you can become exposed to several major world religions, and probably the most passionately observed of these is Civil War Re-enactments.

Put your rider's bum on his back. A foot will bend just below the belly line, and a head at the end of the spine.

Now we're going to add some gear. Don't worry about over lapping lines - we're going to get messier than this!

Add some eyes, nose and head gear. We'll connect the dots next and give him some flashy mane.

Time for s'more gear. Blankets, straps, stirrups, and saddle can go in here.

I don't like where my chin strap ended up, but that's OK. Like anything else, we'll have a chance to change it later.

(Told you we were going to get messy.)

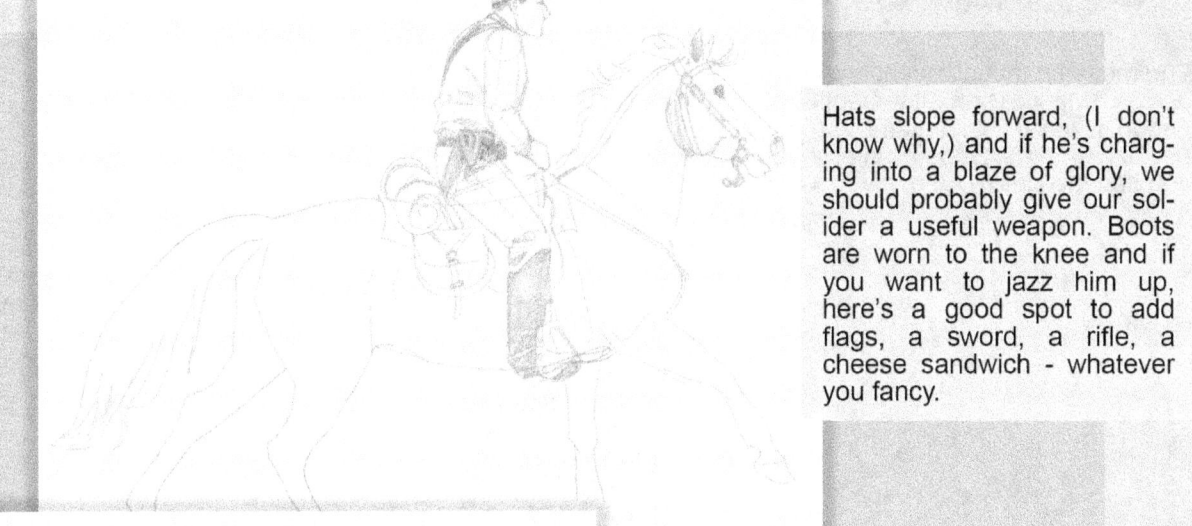

Hats slope forward, (I don't know why,) and if he's charging into a blaze of glory, we should probably give our solider a useful weapon. Boots are worn to the knee and if you want to jazz him up, here's a good spot to add flags, a sword, a rifle, a cheese sandwich - whatever you fancy.

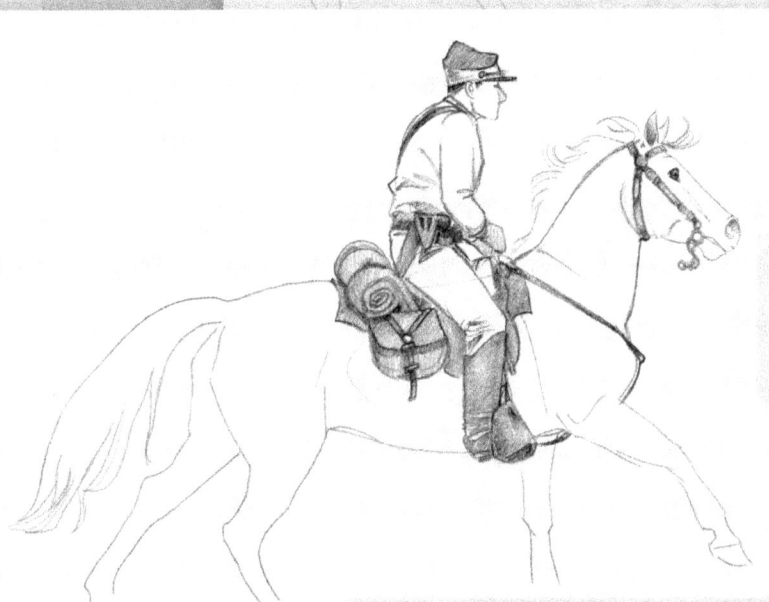

Say, you clean up nice! Take your kneaded eraser and get rid of those pesky lines you don't need.

Don't have a silent tantrum if everything isn't just *exactly* right. We can hide it with some shadows or by pressing harder with our pencil to get that defining dark line.

Sound the bugle! This wordier series of events has resulted in a gentleman on a fine steed you can be proud of.

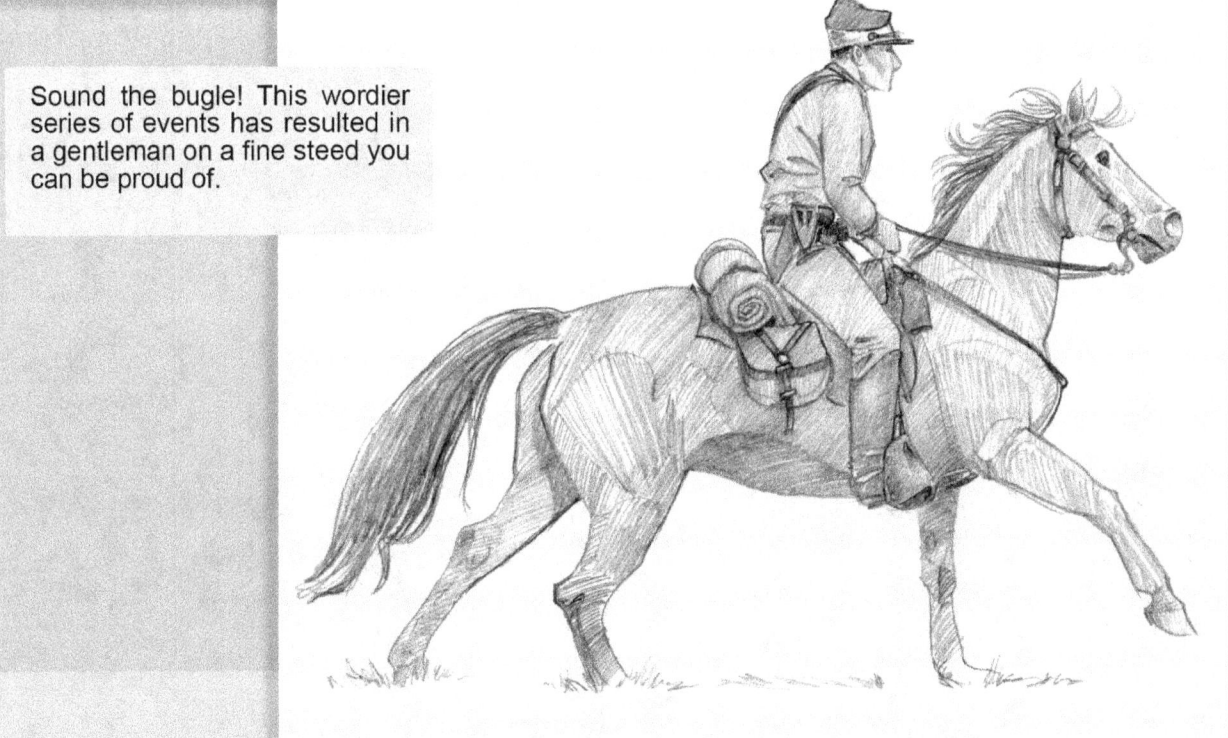

OREGON TRAIL

The movement of pioneers westward across America is an oft romanticized period. It was a vast, untamed region, unclaimed by anybody, unless you counted the Native Americans, which these hardy pioneers did not.

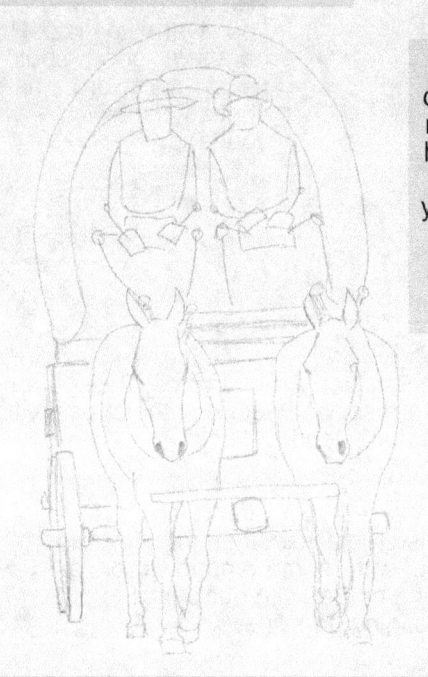

If you can tackle a circle, triangle, and rectangle, you can handle a team and wagon. Start with your basic stick figures and shapes. Don't be afraid to get messy.

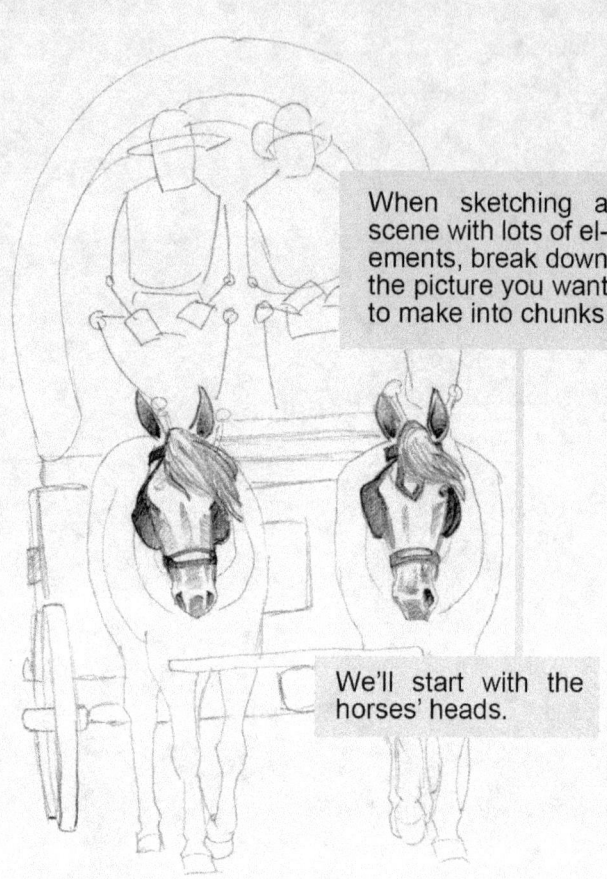

When sketching a scene with lots of elements, break down the picture you want to make into chunks.

We'll start with the horses' heads.

Next we'll add s'more gear. Everyone needs to accessorize after all.

Add some straps, and build off the collar and headgear you've already done.

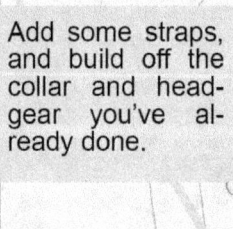

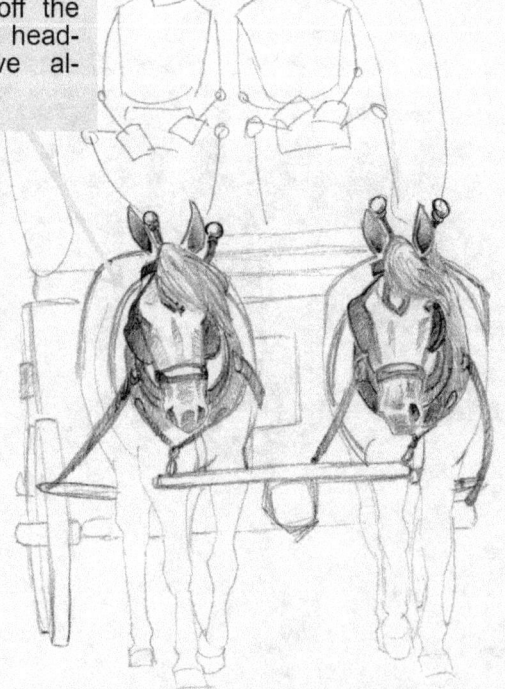

Because of our point of view, the rest of our horses' bodies are pretty easy. Now we can move onto the next chunk.

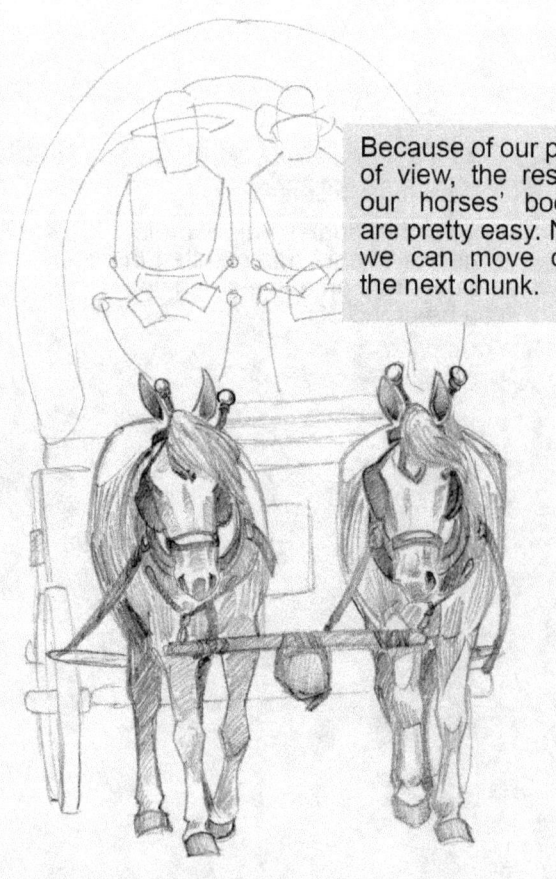

This wagon isn't as hard as it looks - use your pencil to make shadows so that no white is left, and then darken lines and axle. Just keep the wheels on the outside and you'll be fine.

Let's be kind to our driver and let him sit in the shade. Don't be afraid to sit him close to his neighbor.

Go ahead and draw over your stick figure. Like any road trip, you spend enough time in a small space with someone, you're going to cross a few lines.

Make a loose 'X' between the team and circle where they cross.

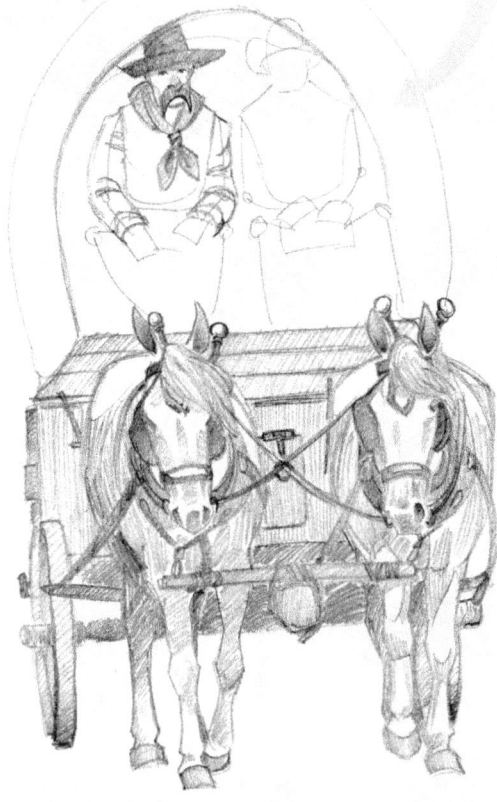

Time to clean up. Erase those lines you don't need and touch up with pencil or ink.

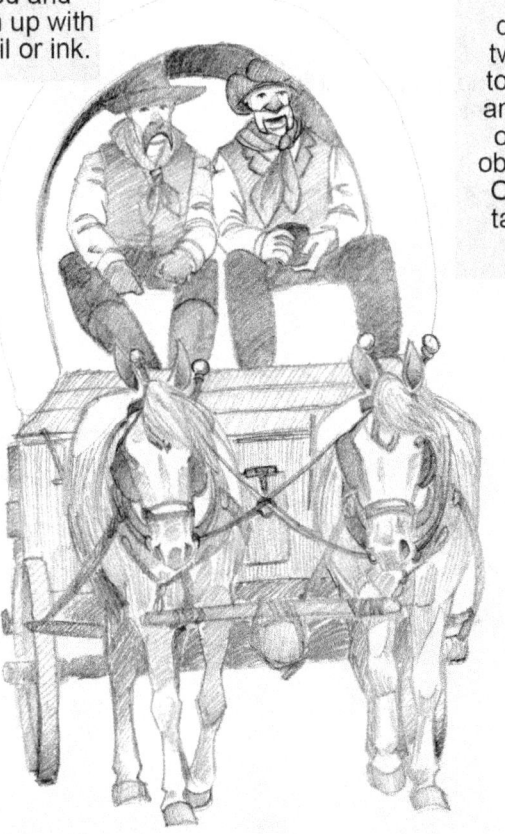

And you're done! These two are ready to set up shop and paint birds on inanimate objects. (This is Oregon we're talking about, after all.)

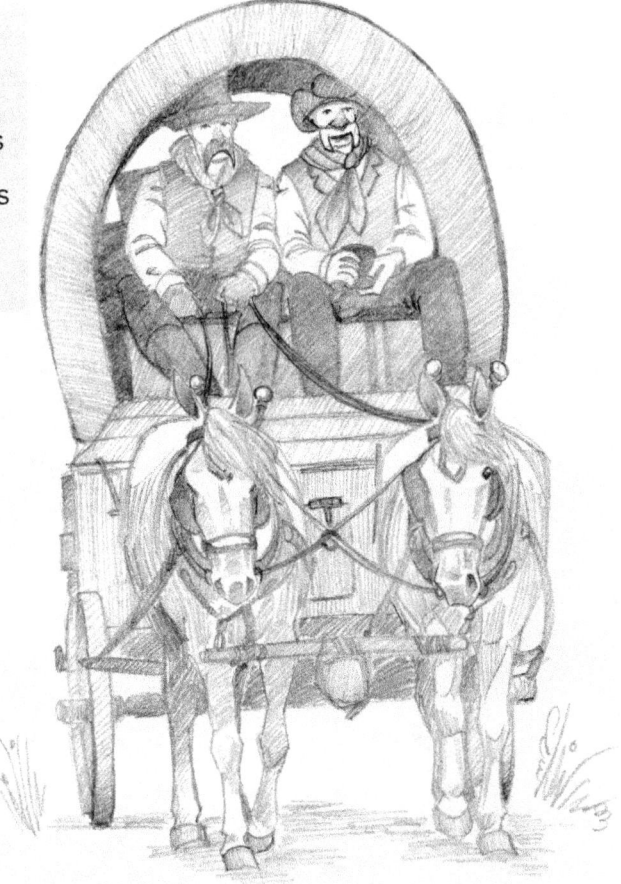

RUSSIAN TROIKA

Russia is one of those cold, tragic romances that produce the kinds of submarine commanders who speak like Scotsmen. For a very long time in Russia, even if you were on the bottom rung of society, if you worked hard, proved to be a team player, and followed the rules, eventually you fell off the bottom rung and snuffed it.

Historically, Russia operated under the "Crazy Homicidal Tyrannical Dictator" system of government who used torture and beheading as the solution to every problem, including fog. But this system has built quite an empire, so I guess the old, popular Russian adage applies, "Don't knock it... cuz you'll be drug out into the street and shot."

Use your guides to make 3 horses, left, right, and center. Only the center horse has a collar and arch, but this is all about looks, so we'll pimp them all out later.

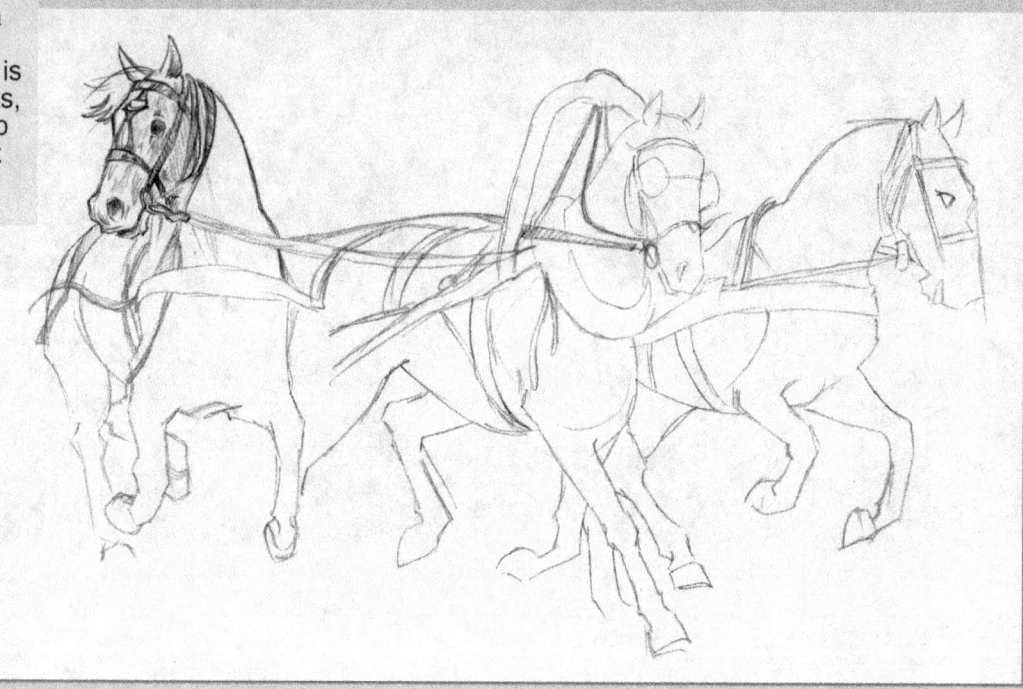

We'll take this in chunks to keep from getting overwhelmed. Start with our horse who leans to the left - he needs gear. Study the bridle and other accessories; we'll be using them again later.

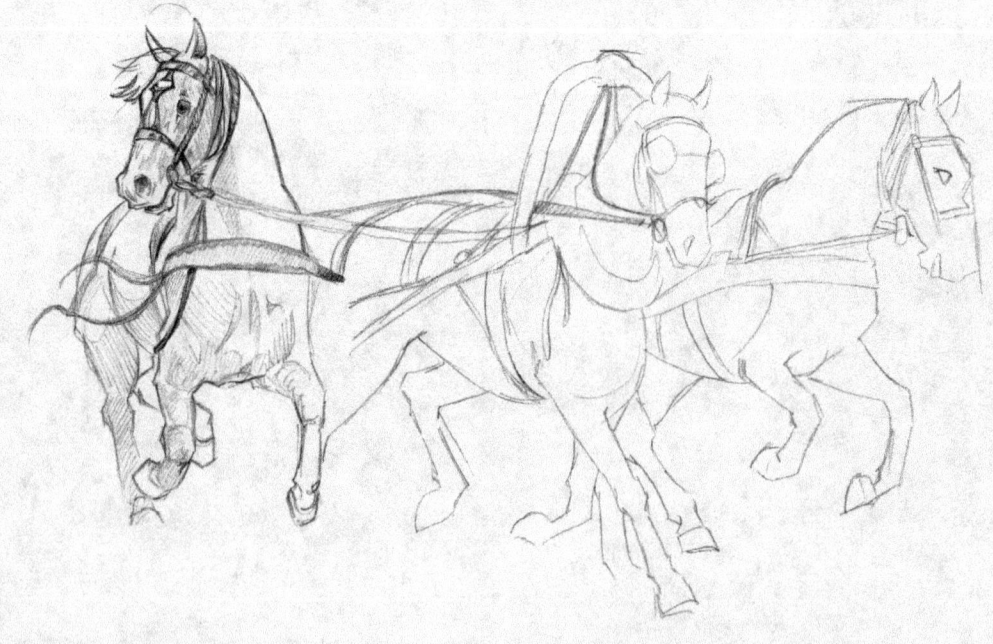

The harnesses for our left and right horses mimic each other, but our center steed has some new tricks. I've left this example more basic, but feel free to add bells, silver, and whatever else once you're comfortable with how it goes together. The Russians would be proud!

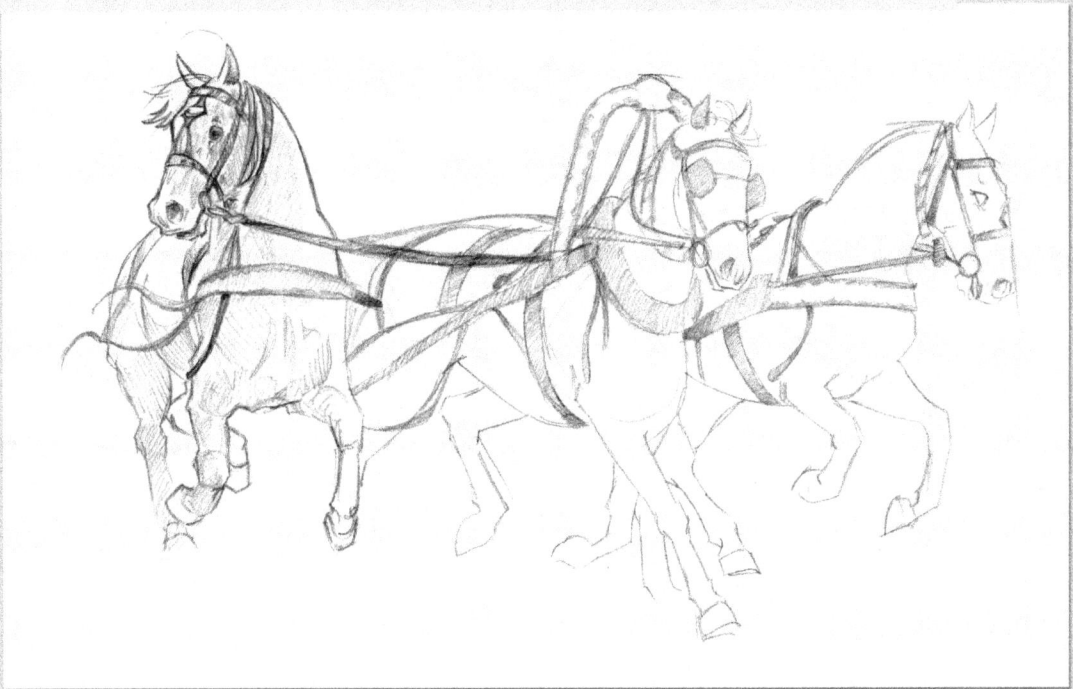

Excellent! Now we have to add some shadows and we're good to go. Erase any lines you don't need, and add some mane if you haven't yet. You can add some blustery snowfall if you like, a handy gel pen is good for that sort of thing, or just leave it as you like it. There you have it, a great troika, and you didn't even have to catch pneumonia!

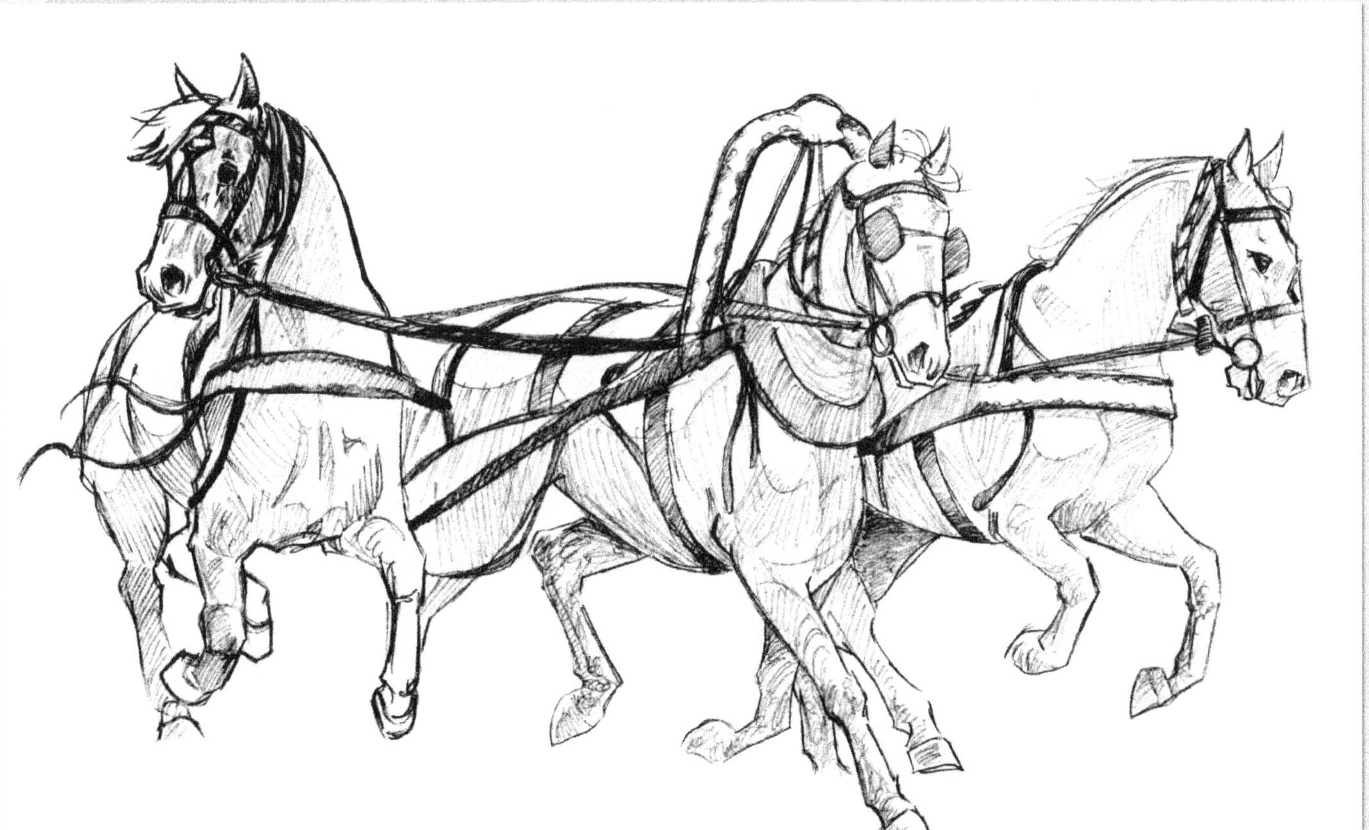

MYTHICAL BEASTS

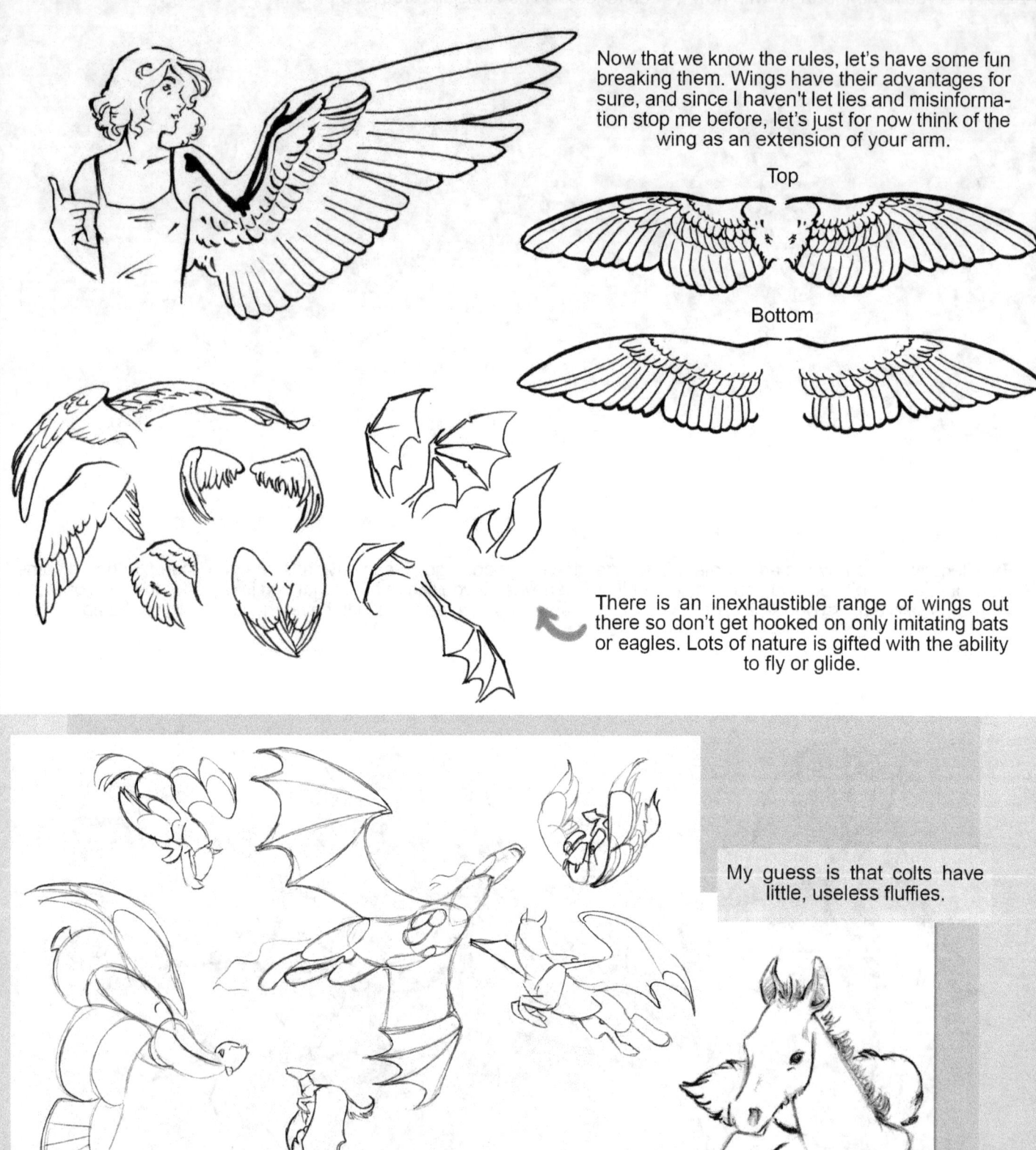

Now that we know the rules, let's have some fun breaking them. Wings have their advantages for sure, and since I haven't let lies and misinformation stop me before, let's just for now think of the wing as an extension of your arm.

Top

Bottom

There is an inexhaustible range of wings out there so don't get hooked on only imitating bats or eagles. Lots of nature is gifted with the ability to fly or glide.

My guess is that colts have little, useless fluffies.

Don't give up on your shapes! They'll be even more helpful since you're adding more to the anatomy.

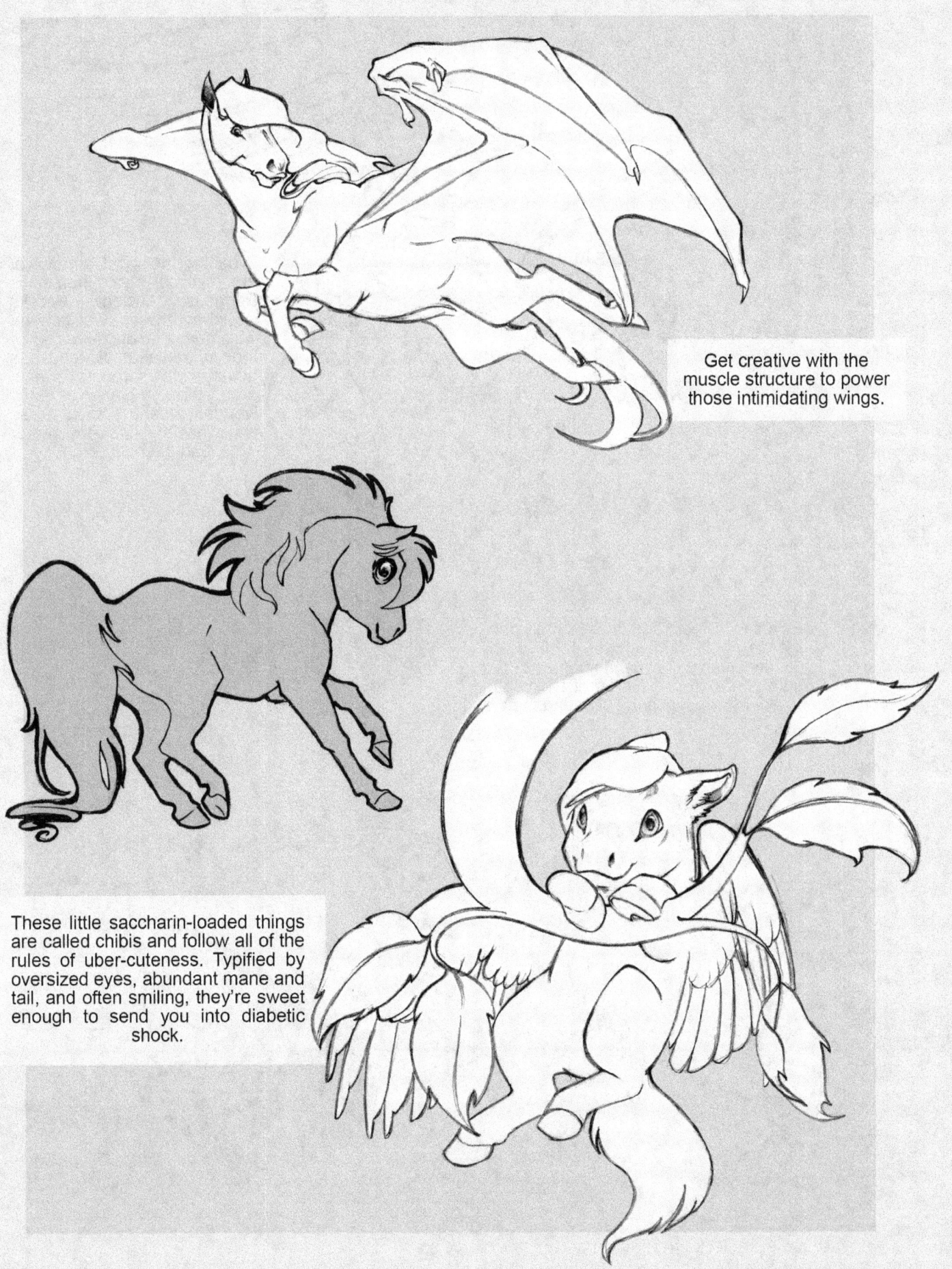

Get creative with the muscle structure to power those intimidating wings.

These little saccharin-loaded things are called chibis and follow all of the rules of uber-cuteness. Typified by oversized eyes, abundant mane and tail, and often smiling, they're sweet enough to send you into diabetic shock.

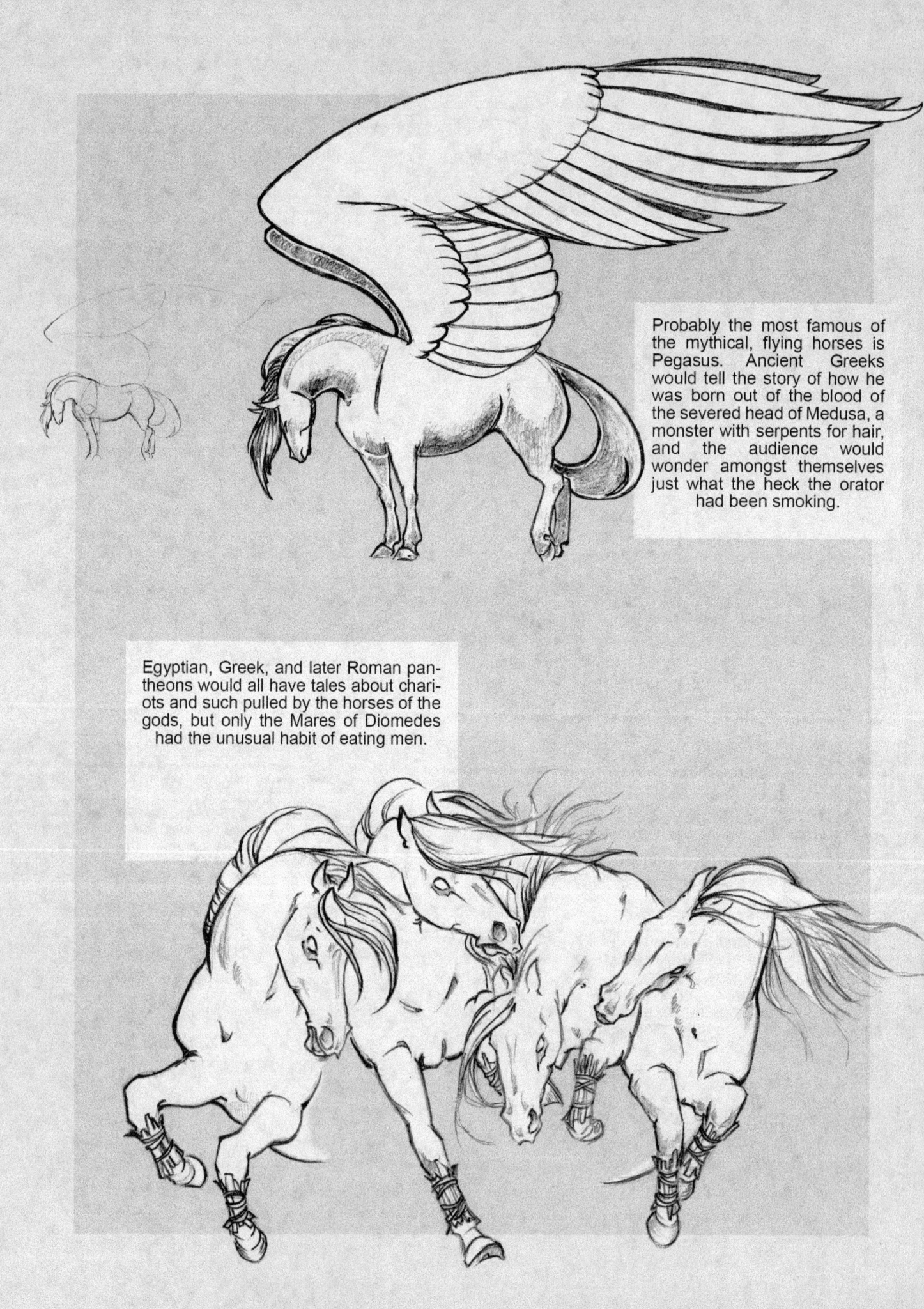

Probably the most famous of the mythical, flying horses is Pegasus. Ancient Greeks would tell the story of how he was born out of the blood of the severed head of Medusa, a monster with serpents for hair, and the audience would wonder amongst themselves just what the heck the orator had been smoking.

Egyptian, Greek, and later Roman pantheons would all have tales about chariots and such pulled by the horses of the gods, but only the Mares of Diomedes had the unusual habit of eating men.

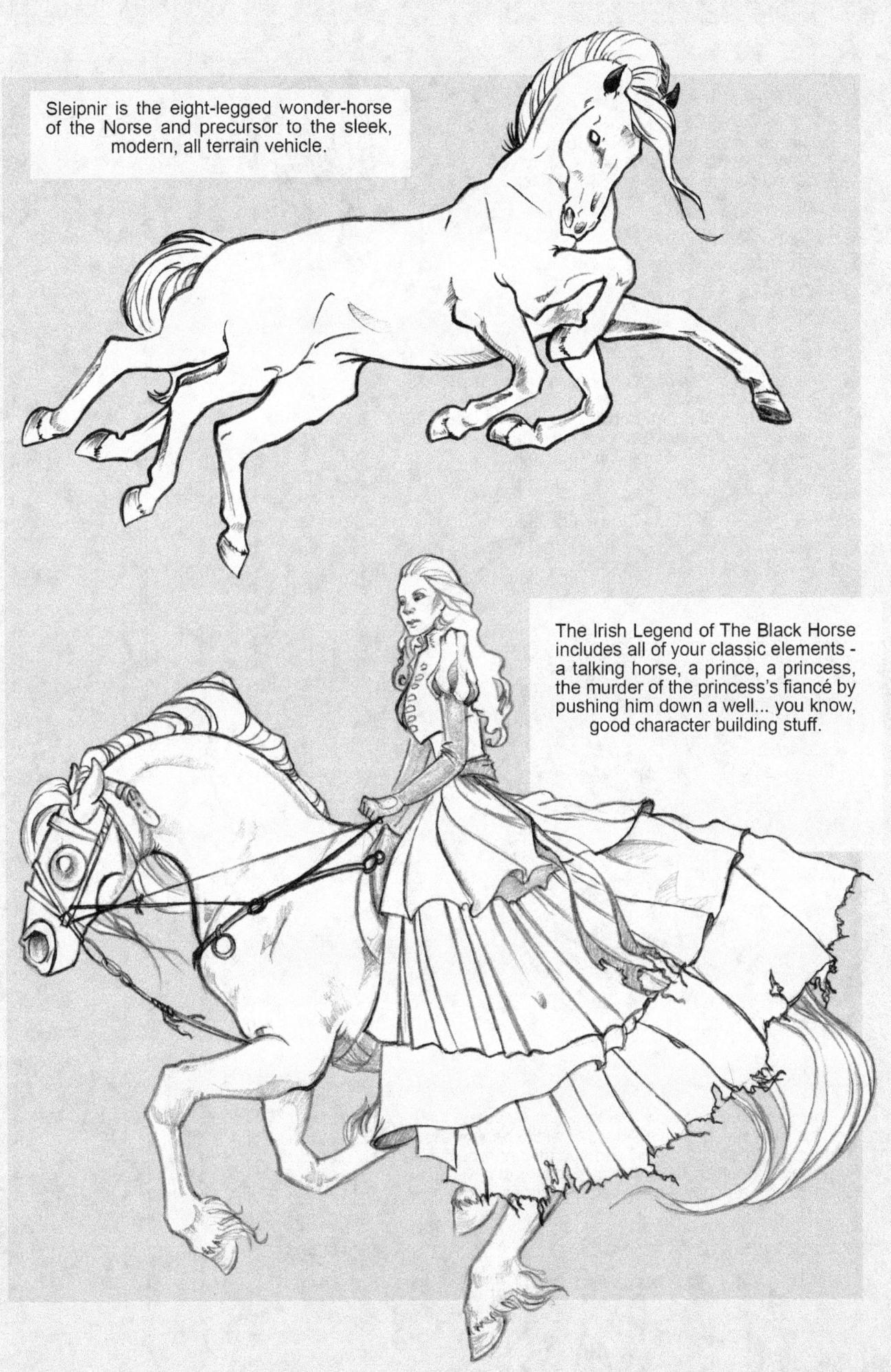

Sleipnir is the eight-legged wonder-horse of the Norse and precursor to the sleek, modern, all terrain vehicle.

The Irish Legend of The Black Horse includes all of your classic elements - a talking horse, a prince, a princess, the murder of the princess's fiancé by pushing him down a well... you know, good character building stuff.

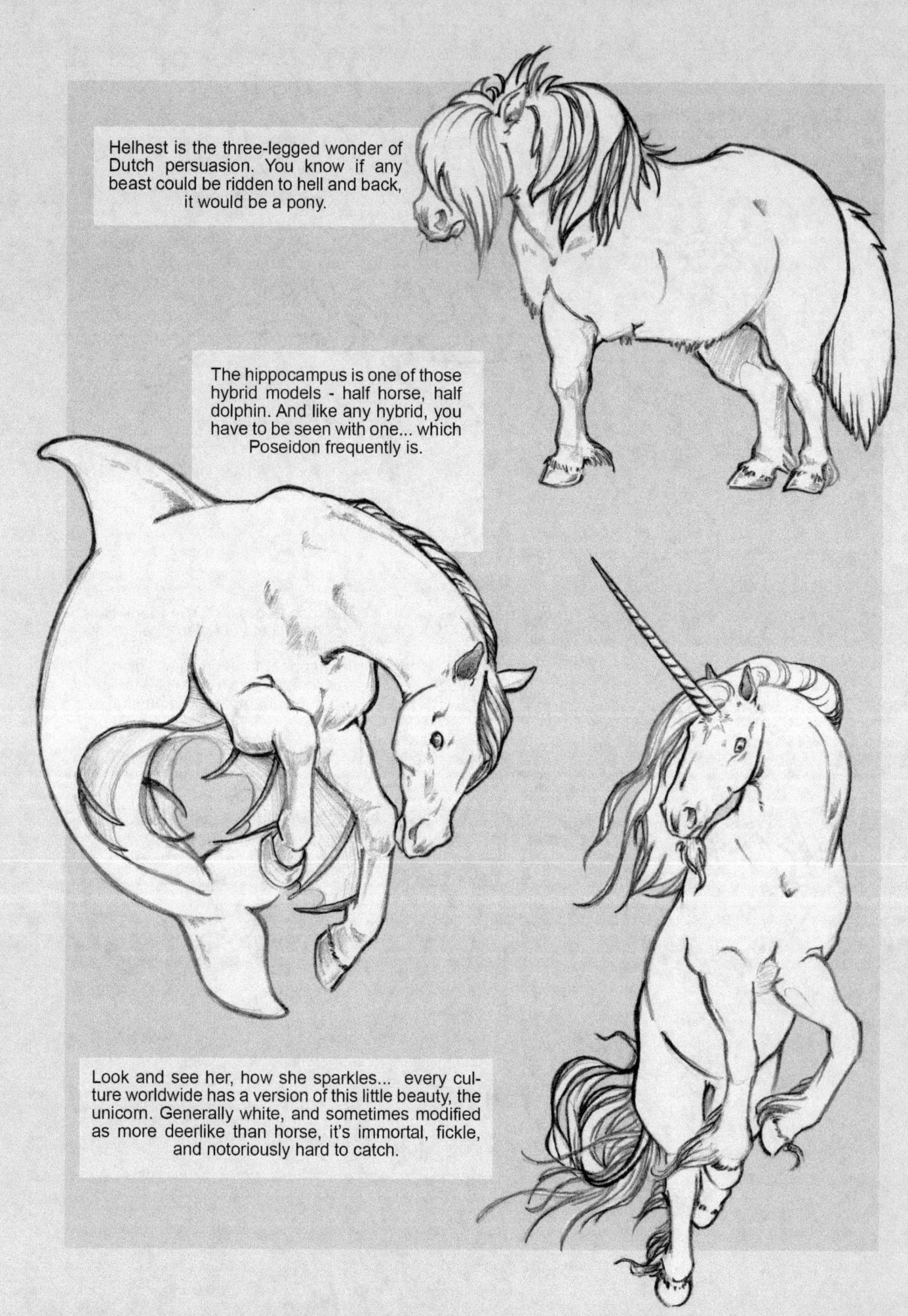

Helhest is the three-legged wonder of Dutch persuasion. You know if any beast could be ridden to hell and back, it would be a pony.

The hippocampus is one of those hybrid models - half horse, half dolphin. And like any hybrid, you have to be seen with one... which Poseidon frequently is.

Look and see her, how she sparkles... every culture worldwide has a version of this little beauty, the unicorn. Generally white, and sometimes modified as more deerlike than horse, it's immortal, fickle, and notoriously hard to catch.

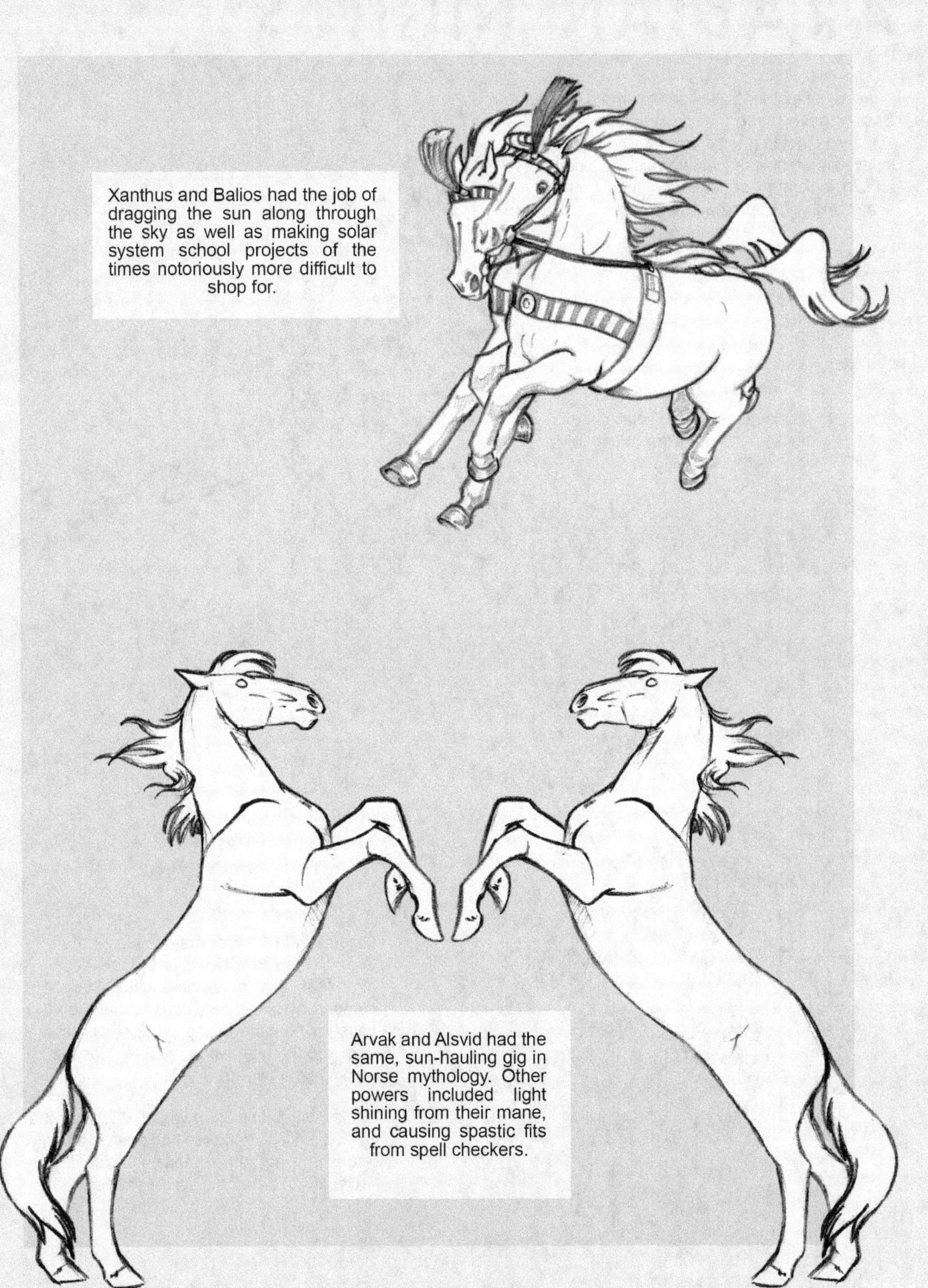

Xanthus and Balios had the job of dragging the sun along through the sky as well as making solar system school projects of the times notoriously more difficult to shop for.

Arvak and Alsvid had the same, sun-hauling gig in Norse mythology. Other powers included light shining from their mane, and causing spastic fits from spell checkers.

ARABIAN NIGHTS

They're not just for Halloween anymore. Costume classes have made there way into horse shows worldwide, not to mention movies, comic cons, cosplay, and renaissance festivals, so your horse should look the part. A really good outfit is not something you pop down to the shops for and take off the rack. You're going to have to make it, so start with the tack you know, and go from there with your imagination.

(If all else fails, douse your horse in glitter and call him a sexy vampire.)

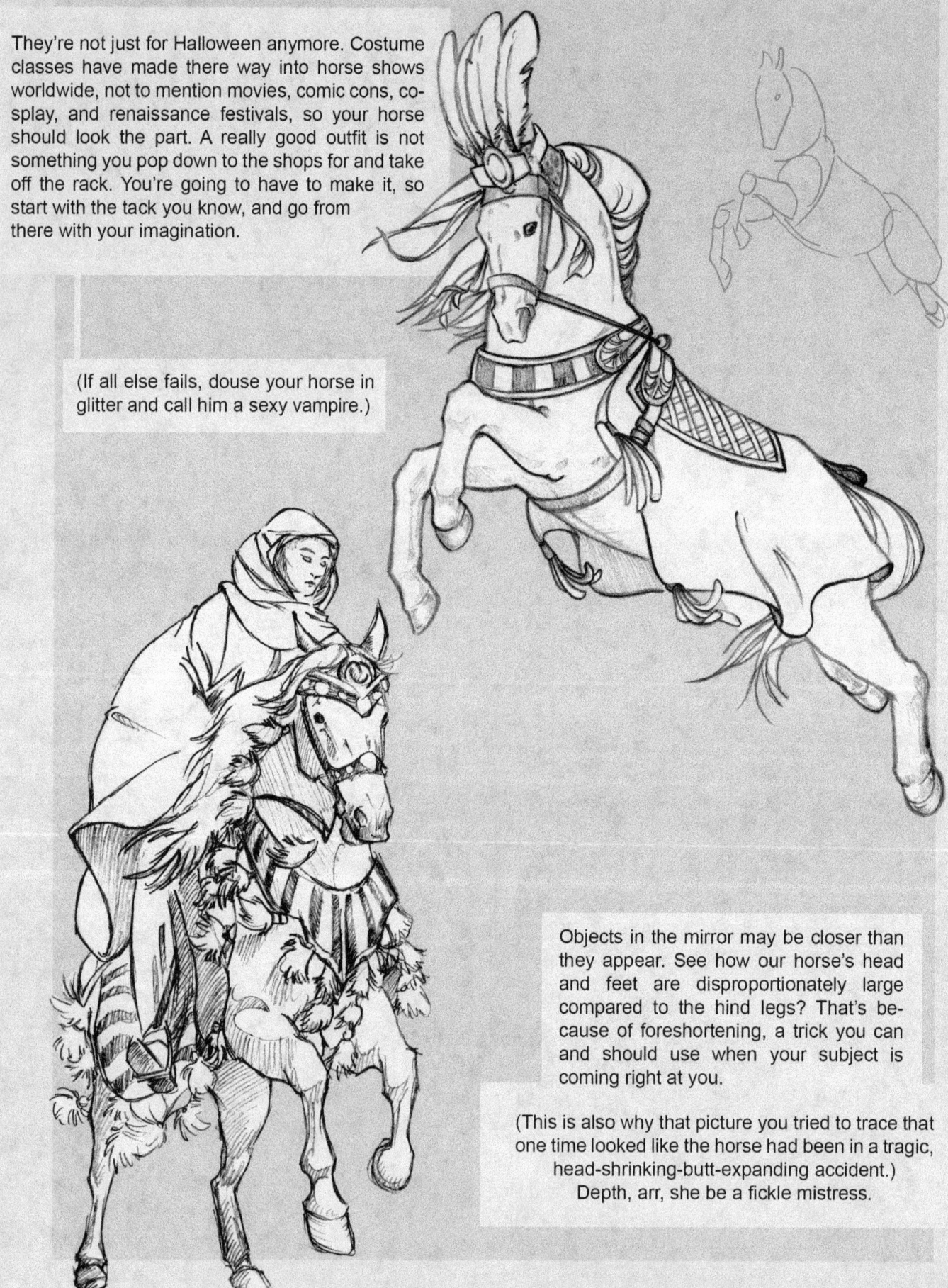

Objects in the mirror may be closer than they appear. See how our horse's head and feet are disproportionately large compared to the hind legs? That's because of foreshortening, a trick you can and should use when your subject is coming right at you.

(This is also why that picture you tried to trace that one time looked like the horse had been in a tragic, head-shrinking-butt-expanding accident.)
Depth, arr, she be a fickle mistress.

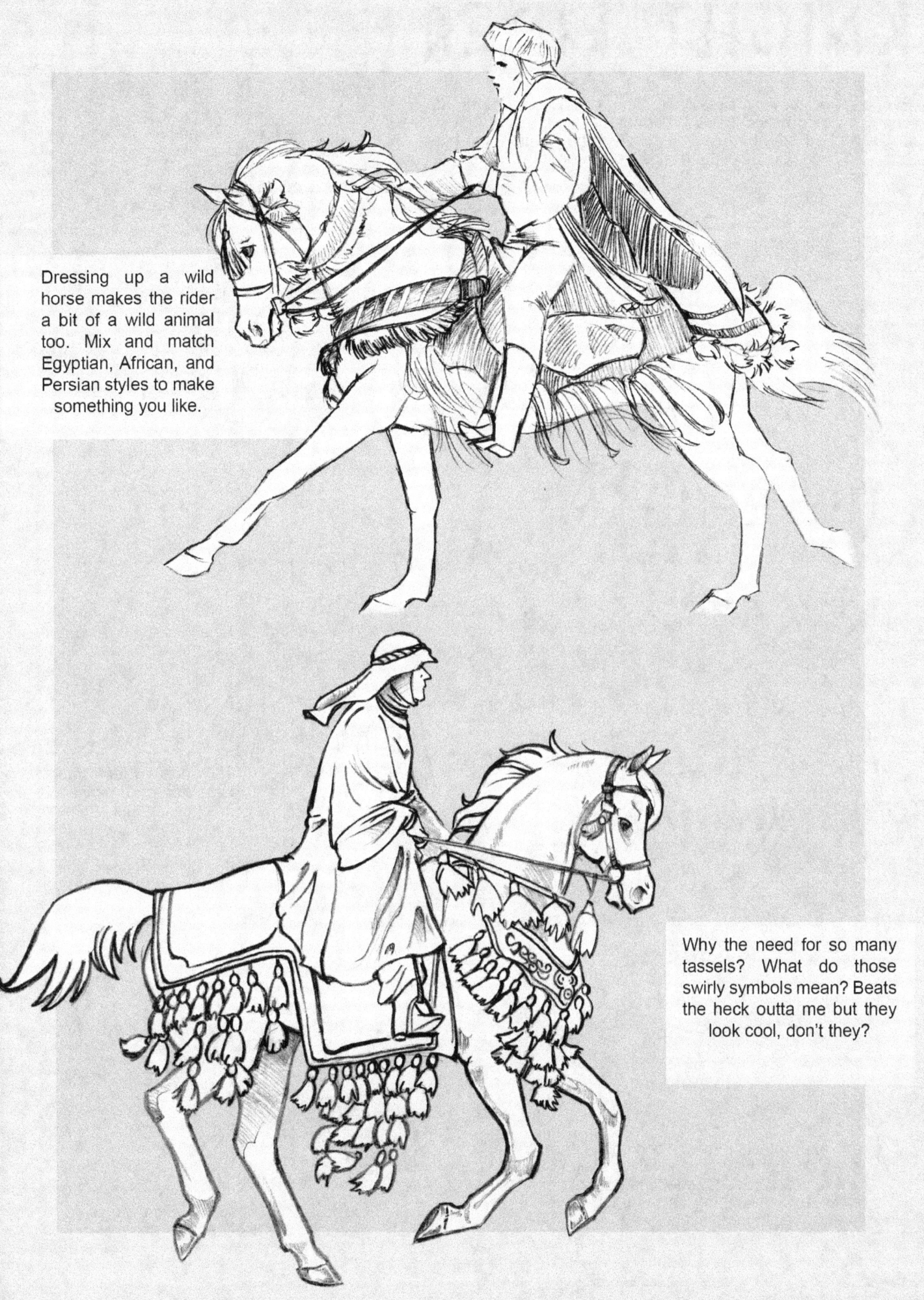

Dressing up a wild horse makes the rider a bit of a wild animal too. Mix and match Egyptian, African, and Persian styles to make something you like.

Why the need for so many tassels? What do those swirly symbols mean? Beats the heck outta me but they look cool, don't they?

KNIGHT RIDER

Barding is armor for horses, there, your useless fact for the day. There is no one-style-fits-all for armor, because this is all hand-made, and suited the protection needs of the location and times, so once you know the basics, go as wild as you like.

Next we have the saddle, but not one the average person would recognize. This is made for holding the rider on, not for comfort.

Start with your noble steed.

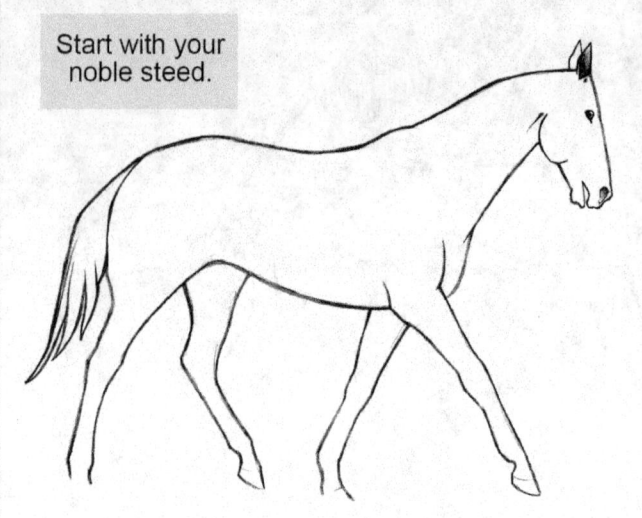

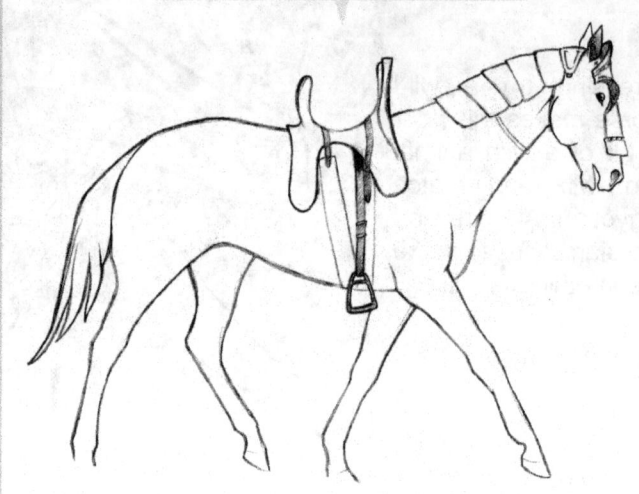

A champron, or champion, protects your horse's face.

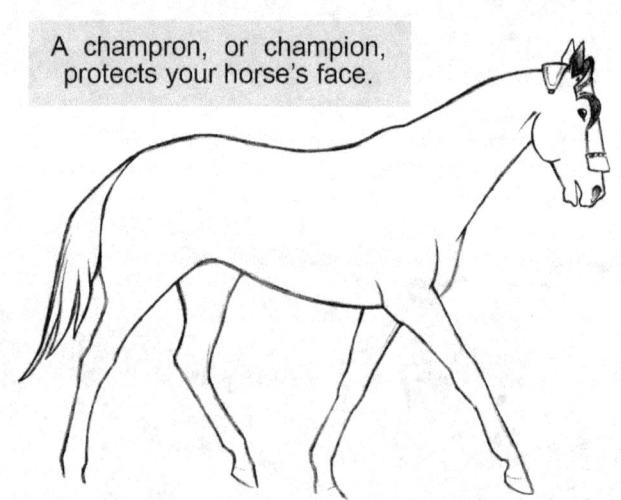

Crupper protects your horse's arse. Combinations of plate, leather, or chain were popular.

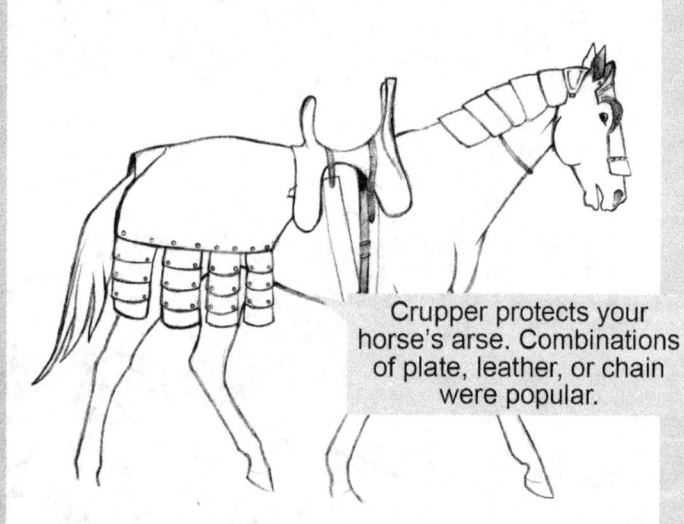

Criniere protects the neck and connects to the champron. It often involves chain-mail, and wrapped around the horse's neck, but I'm keeping it simple. Criniet light for this tutorial.

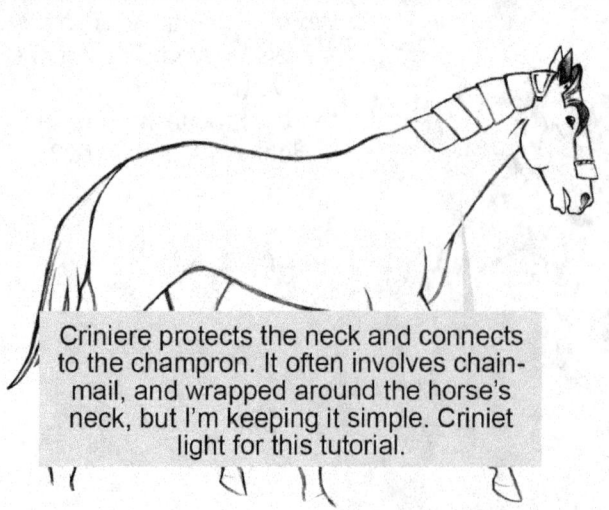

Peytral is for chest protection and can also be made of various materials.

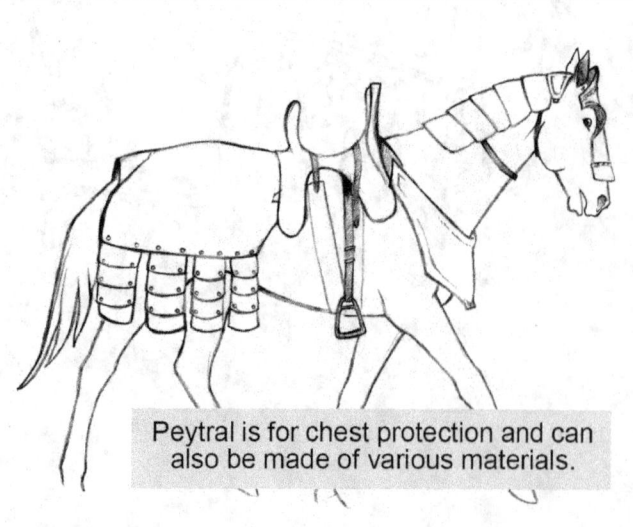

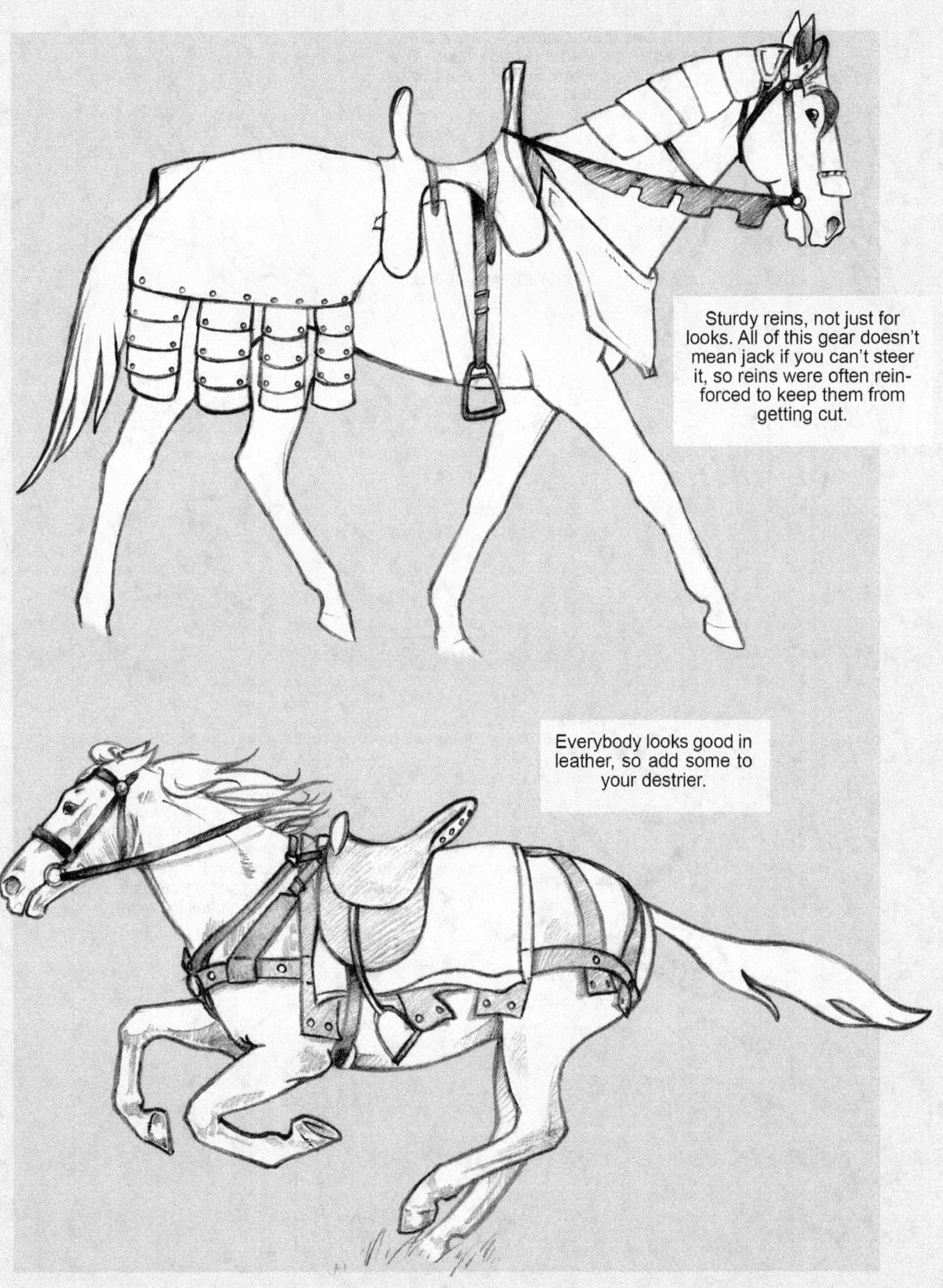

Sturdy reins, not just for looks. All of this gear doesn't mean jack if you can't steer it, so reins were often reinforced to keep them from getting cut.

Everybody looks good in leather, so add some to your destrier.

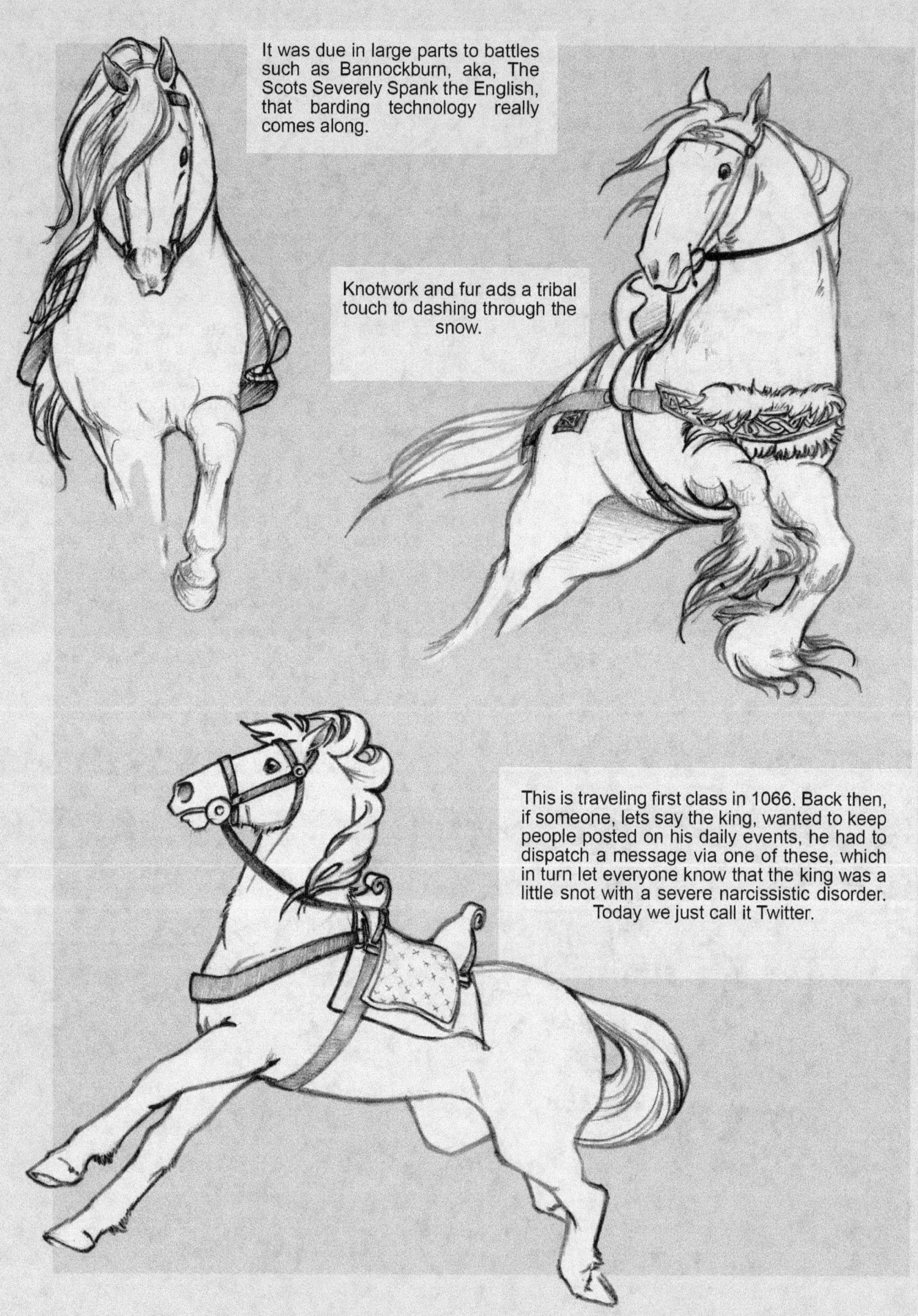

It was due in large parts to battles such as Bannockburn, aka, The Scots Severely Spank the English, that barding technology really comes along.

Knotwork and fur ads a tribal touch to dashing through the snow.

This is traveling first class in 1066. Back then, if someone, lets say the king, wanted to keep people posted on his daily events, he had to dispatch a message via one of these, which in turn let everyone know that the king was a little snot with a severe narcissistic disorder. Today we just call it Twitter.

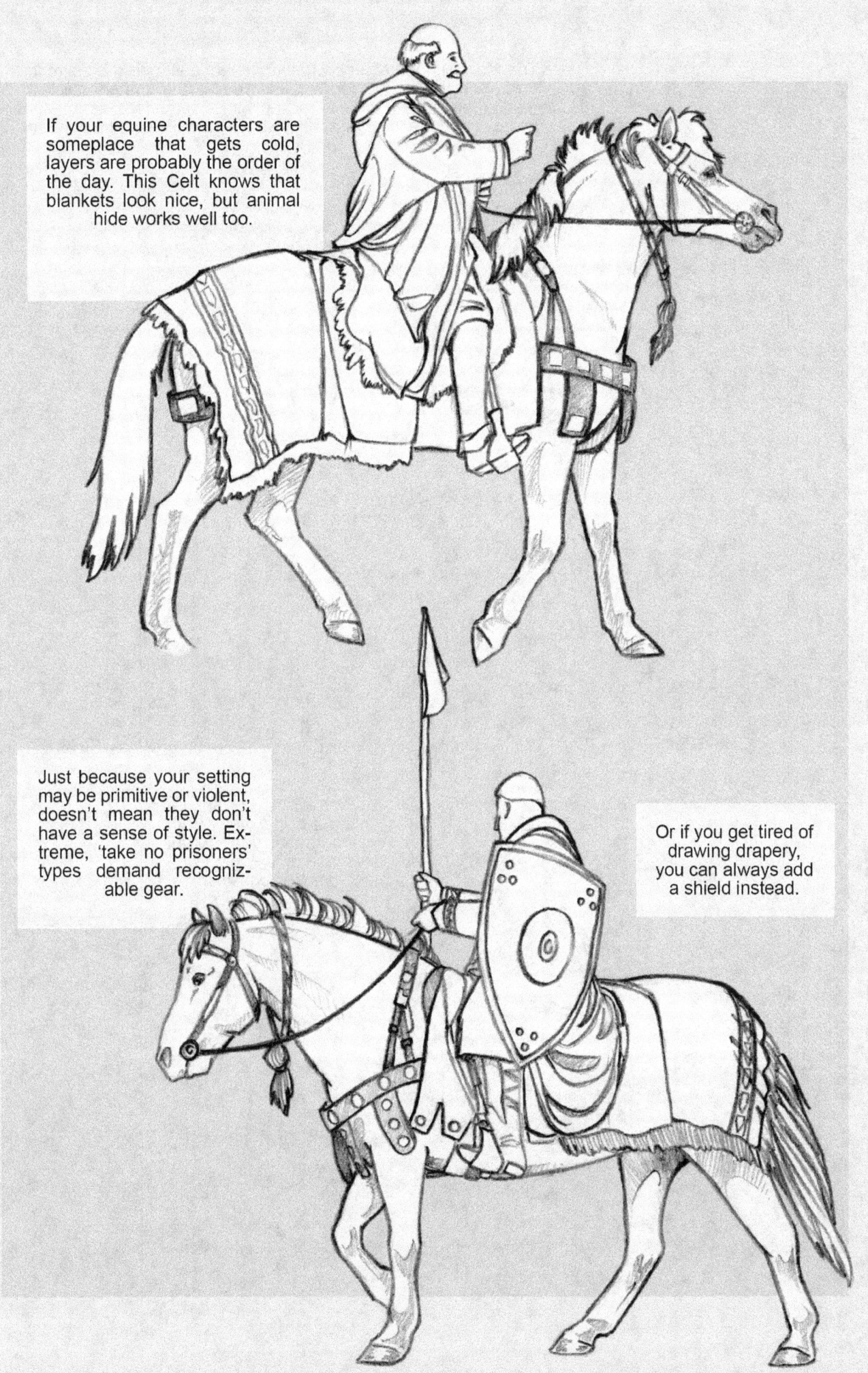

If your equine characters are someplace that gets cold, layers are probably the order of the day. This Celt knows that blankets look nice, but animal hide works well too.

Just because your setting may be primitive or violent, doesn't mean they don't have a sense of style. Extreme, 'take no prisoners' types demand recognizable gear.

Or if you get tired of drawing drapery, you can always add a shield instead.

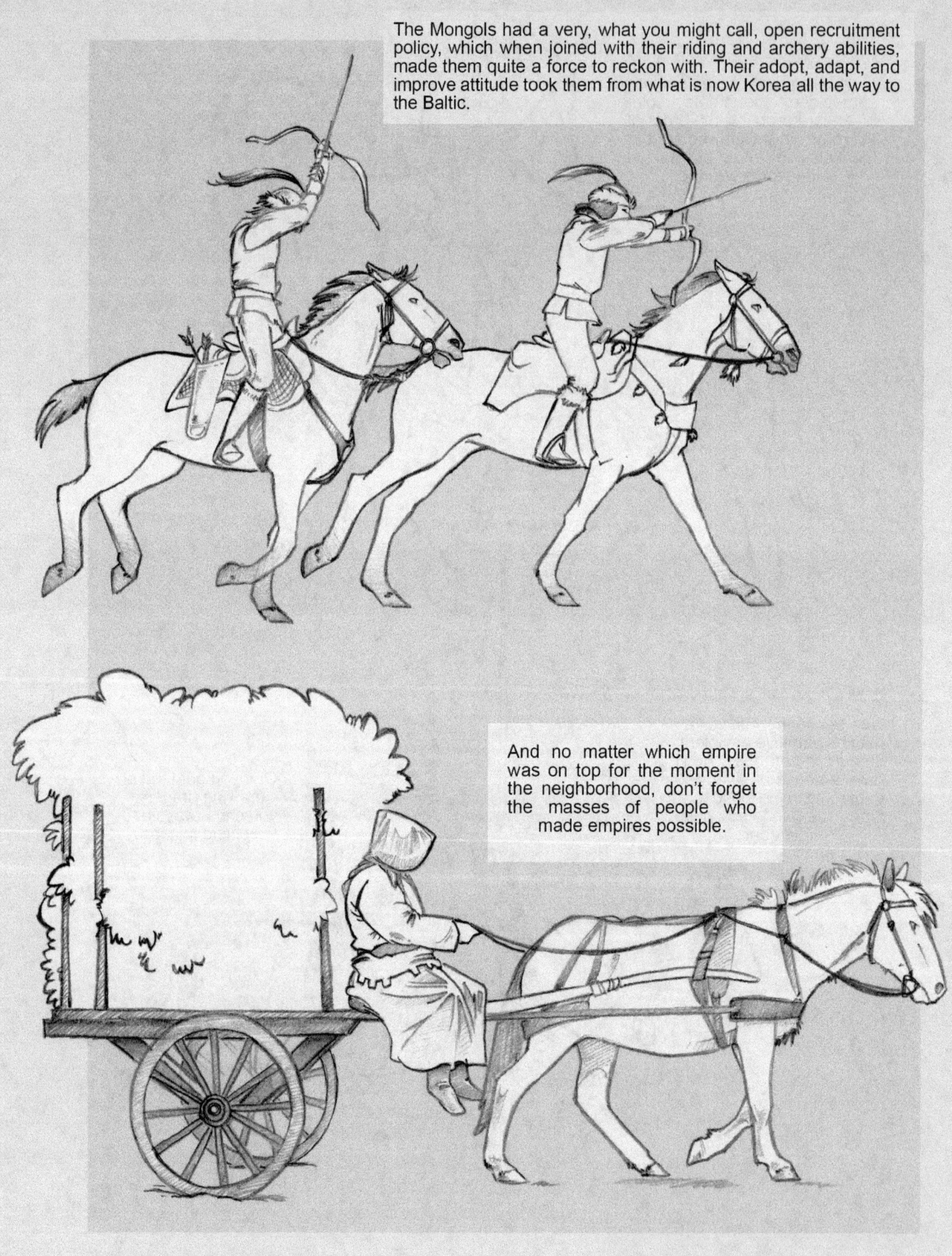

The Mongols had a very, what you might call, open recruitment policy, which when joined with their riding and archery abilities, made them quite a force to reckon with. Their adopt, adapt, and improve attitude took them from what is now Korea all the way to the Baltic.

And no matter which empire was on top for the moment in the neighborhood, don't forget the masses of people who made empires possible.

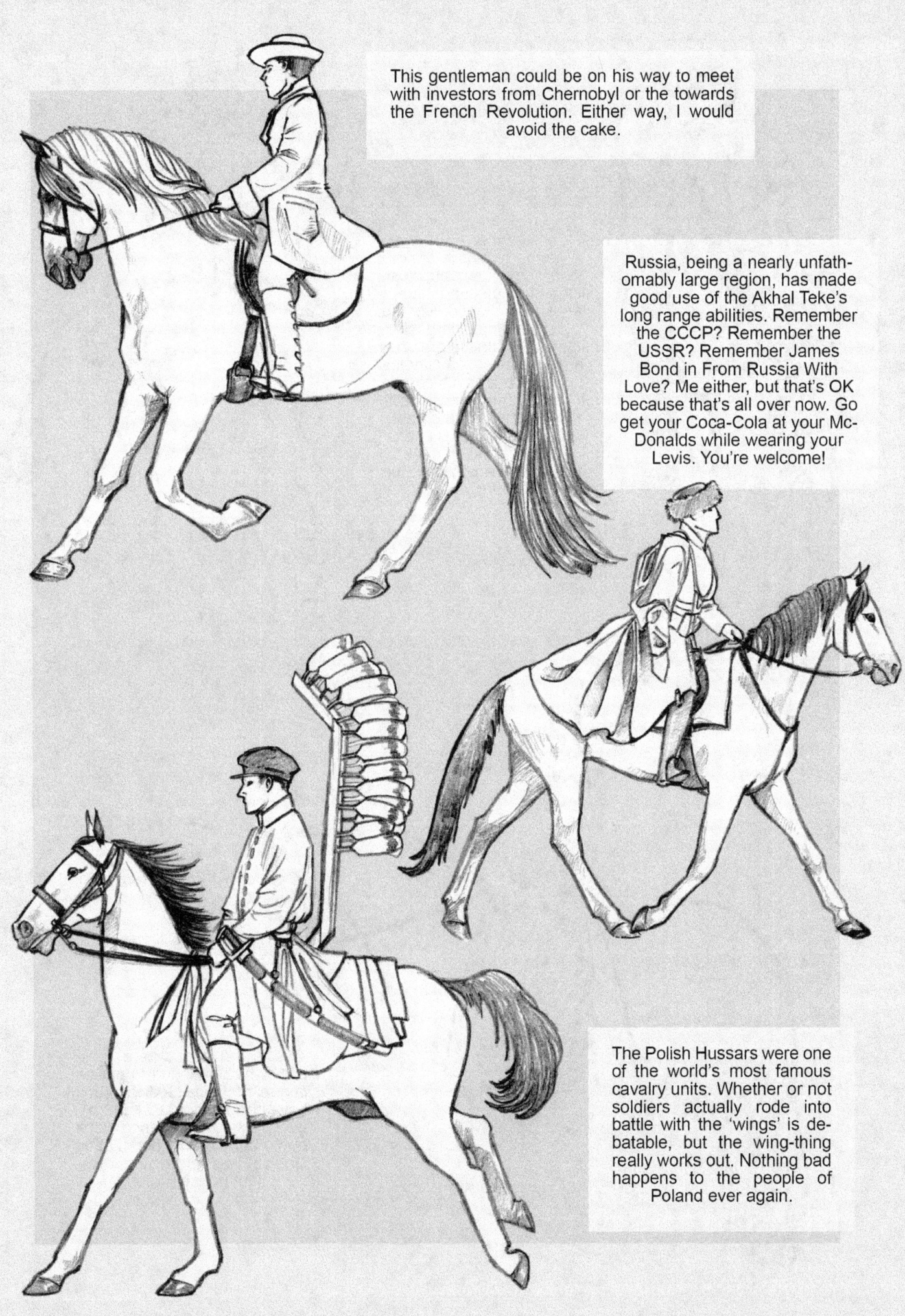

This gentleman could be on his way to meet with investors from Chernobyl or the towards the French Revolution. Either way, I would avoid the cake.

Russia, being a nearly unfathomably large region, has made good use of the Akhal Teke's long range abilities. Remember the CCCP? Remember the USSR? Remember James Bond in From Russia With Love? Me either, but that's OK because that's all over now. Go get your Coca-Cola at your McDonalds while wearing your Levis. You're welcome!

The Polish Hussars were one of the world's most famous cavalry units. Whether or not soldiers actually rode into battle with the 'wings' is debatable, but the wing-thing really works out. Nothing bad happens to the people of Poland ever again.

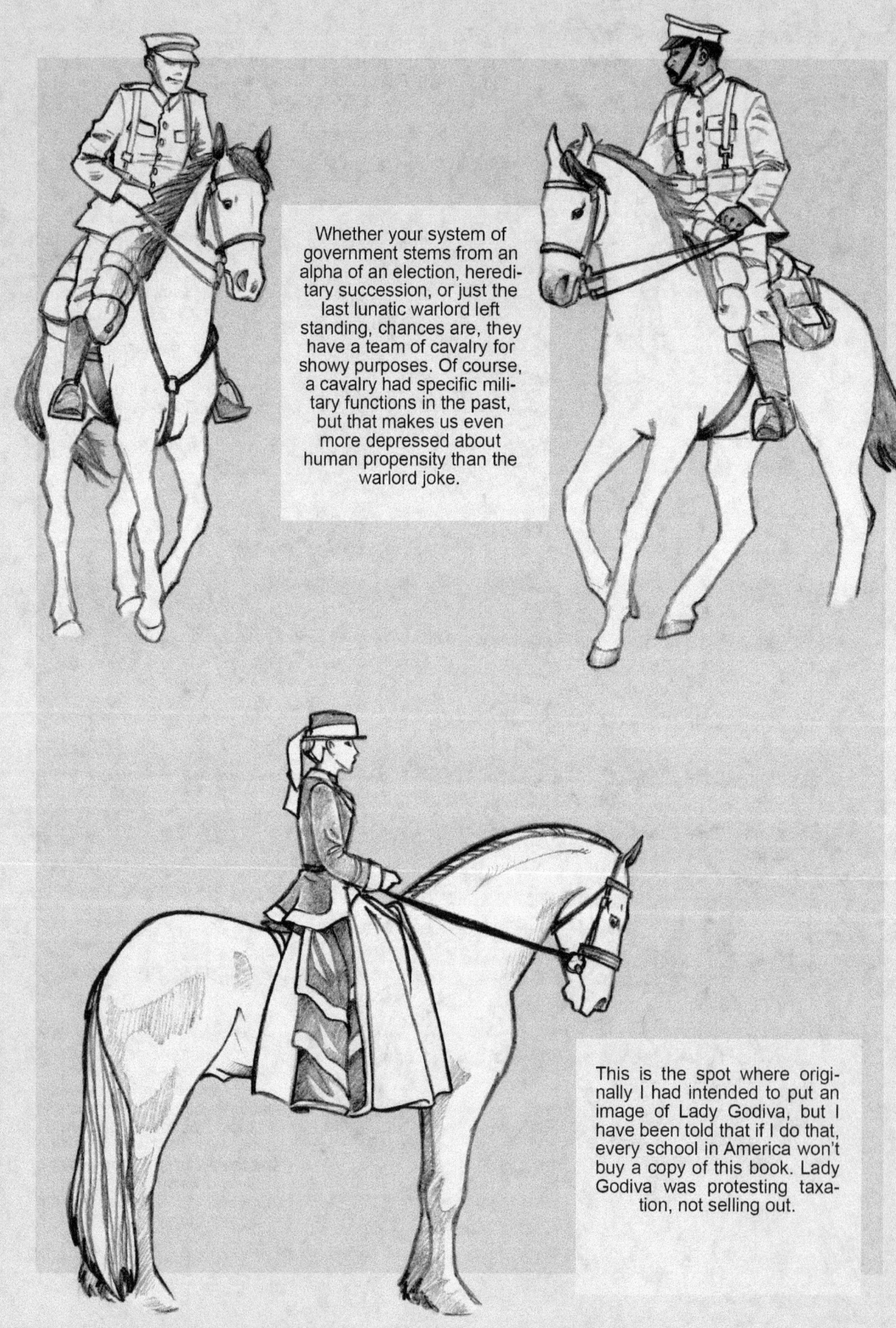

Whether your system of government stems from an alpha of an election, heredi-tary succession, or just the last lunatic warlord left standing, chances are, they have a team of cavalry for showy purposes. Of course, a cavalry had specific mili-tary functions in the past, but that makes us even more depressed about human propensity than the warlord joke.

This is the spot where origi-nally I had intended to put an image of Lady Godiva, but I have been told that if I do that, every school in America won't buy a copy of this book. Lady Godiva was protesting taxa-tion, not selling out.

TRIBAL GEAR

In the days before Customs Check, nations weren't terrifically clever about looking out for native ecological systems. Transplanting species from one place to another on the globe is hardly a new idea, and horses have to be some of the least lethal things brought from old world Europe to the Americas and Australia.

But back to the tribal gear, which is the point of this page if you will remember. Tack has at least one of two functions: Be practical and/or look good. Whether it's a crest, a color, or a pattern, the point is to convey information. Between all the feathers, leather, hides and patterns, you're going to have a blast drawing it.

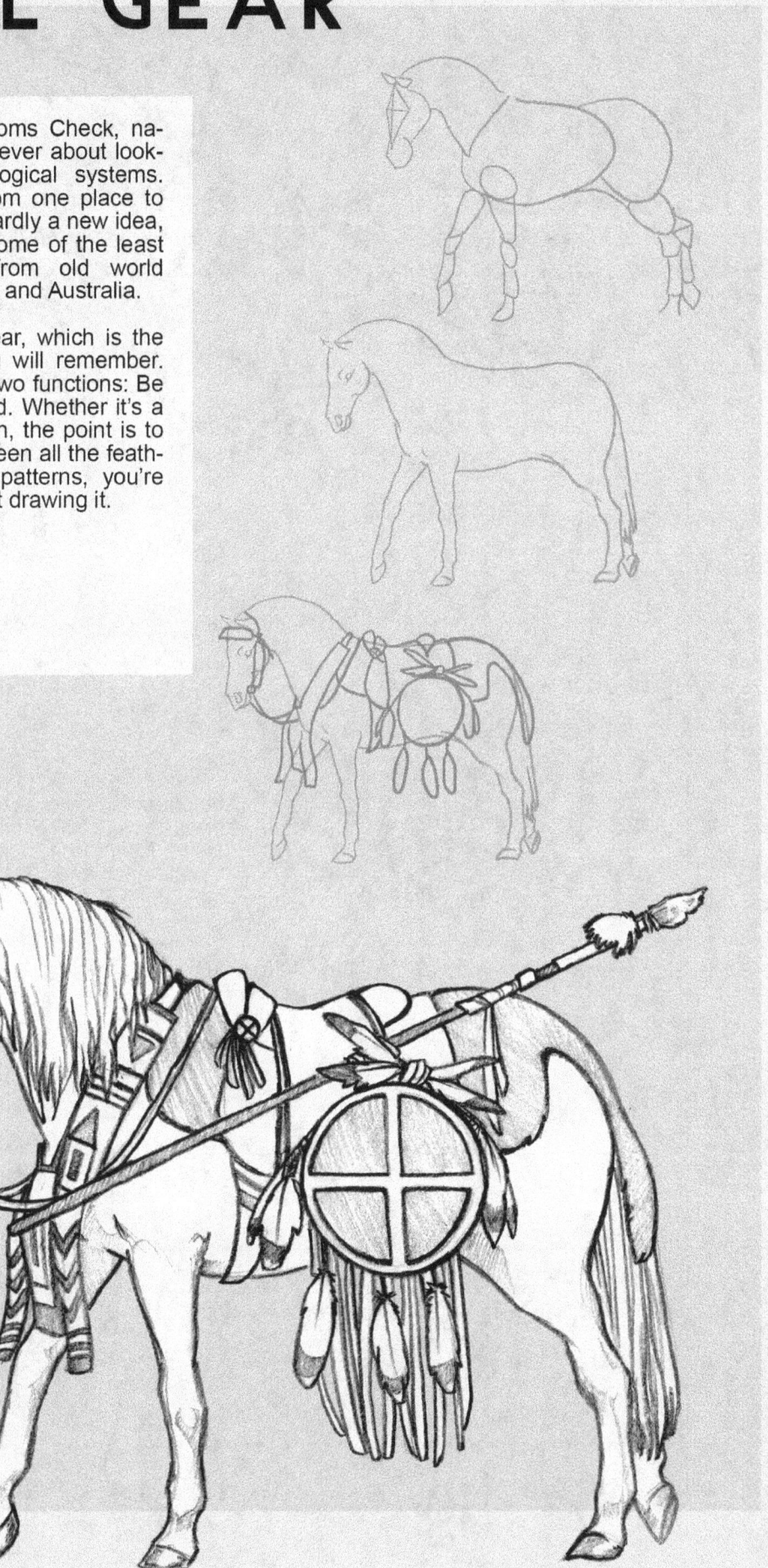

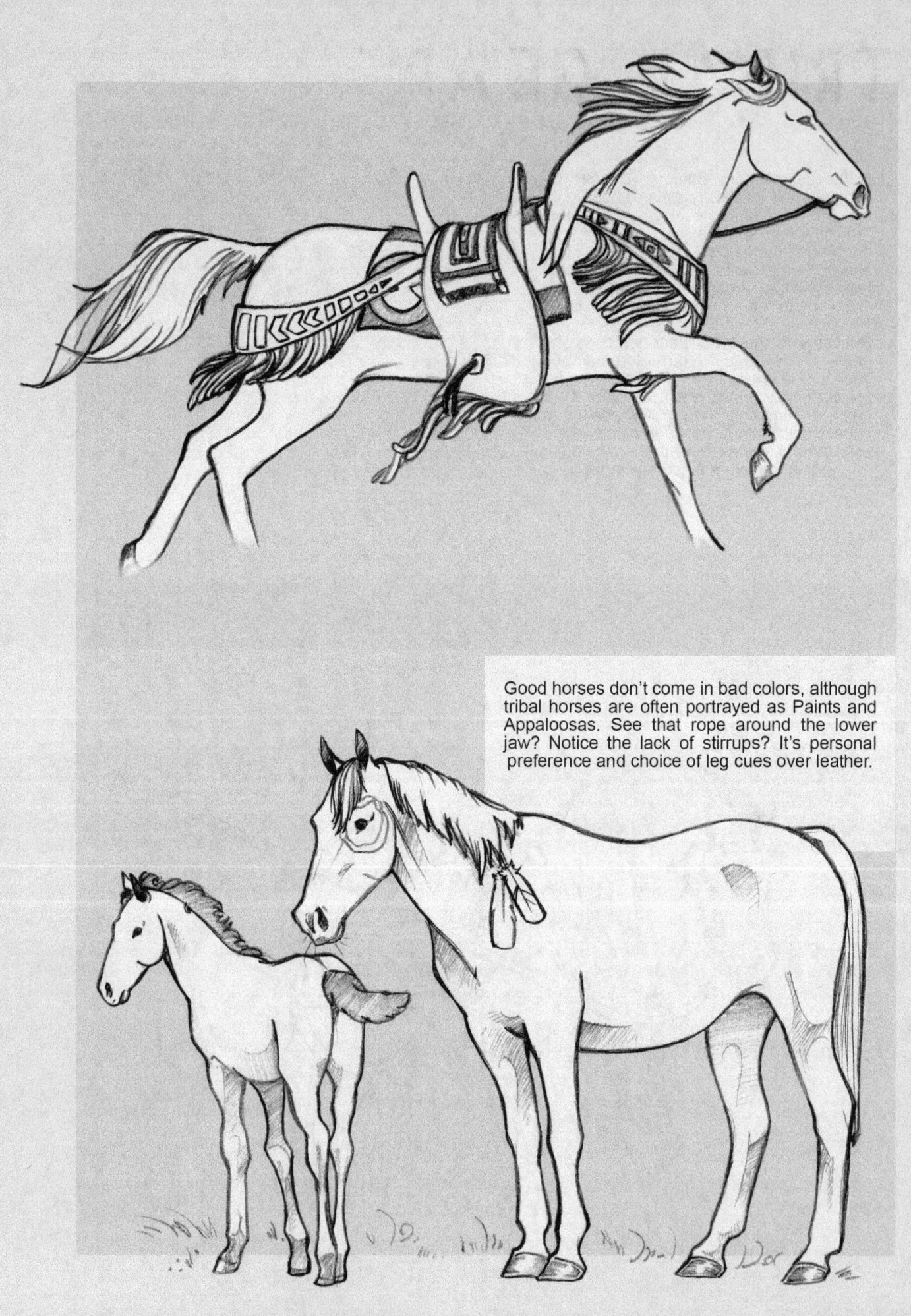

Good horses don't come in bad colors, although tribal horses are often portrayed as Paints and Appaloosas. See that rope around the lower jaw? Notice the lack of stirrups? It's personal preference and choice of leg cues over leather.

SWEET RIDES

Everyone likes a fine, polished, set of wheels, right? Tricking them out is not as intimidating once you know a few things.

HORIZON LINE

VANISHING POINT   VANISHING POINT

I am going to assume the you already know what a horizon line and vanishing points are. A **straight edge** will be helpful here, but if you don't have one, find a book, a folder, an easily inconvenienced sibling, whatever it takes. Any tool can be the right tool.

It's OK to erase and change your lines until you get the flow you want. Don't be afraid to admit the eraser is the most used item in your artistic arsenal. (I sure admit it!)

So let's put practice into use. Which point of perspective do you think this horse and cart are using?

If you said, "None of thee above." Congratulations! It's a one point perspective.

You should add as many guidelines from your vanishing points as you need. After all, you can always erase them later. But now comes something trickier... the wheel. If you have a set of *circle* and *ellipse guides*, along with maybe a few *french curves*, this will be easier for you. If you have no idea what I was just talking about there, don't fret. Your local art supply store will be able to help you, and for the rest of this tutorial, we'll stick with a compass and a pencil.

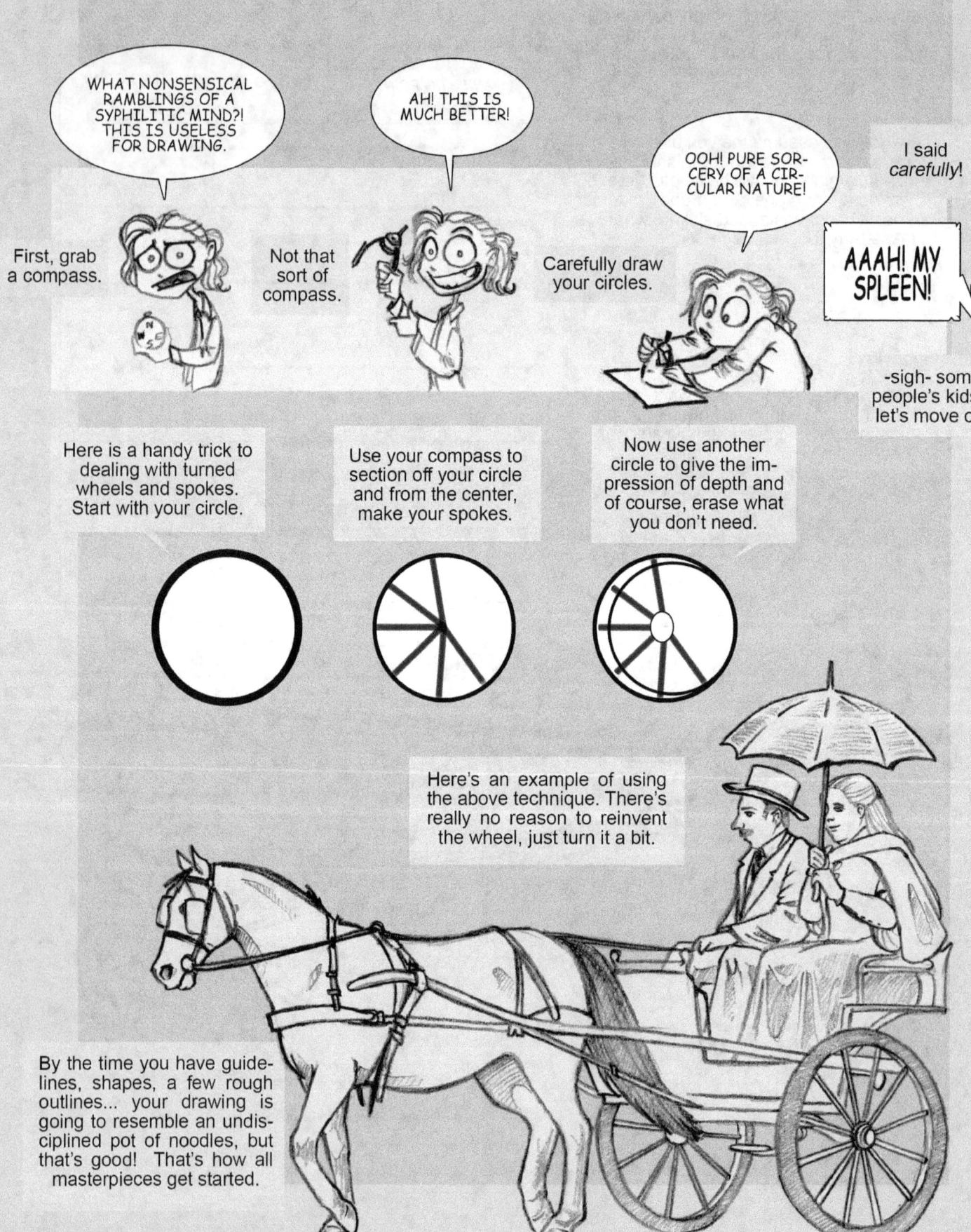

WHAT NONSENSICAL RAMBLINGS OF A SYPHILITIC MIND?! THIS IS USELESS FOR DRAWING.

AH! THIS IS MUCH BETTER!

OOH! PURE SORCERY OF A CIRCULAR NATURE!

I said *carefully*!

AAAH! MY SPLEEN!

First, grab a compass.

Not that sort of compass.

Carefully draw your circles.

-sigh- some people's kids... let's move on.

Here is a handy trick to dealing with turned wheels and spokes. Start with your circle.

Use your compass to section off your circle and from the center, make your spokes.

Now use another circle to give the impression of depth and of course, erase what you don't need.

Here's an example of using the above technique. There's really no reason to reinvent the wheel, just turn it a bit.

By the time you have guidelines, shapes, a few rough outlines... your drawing is going to resemble an undisciplined pot of noodles, but that's good! That's how all masterpieces get started.

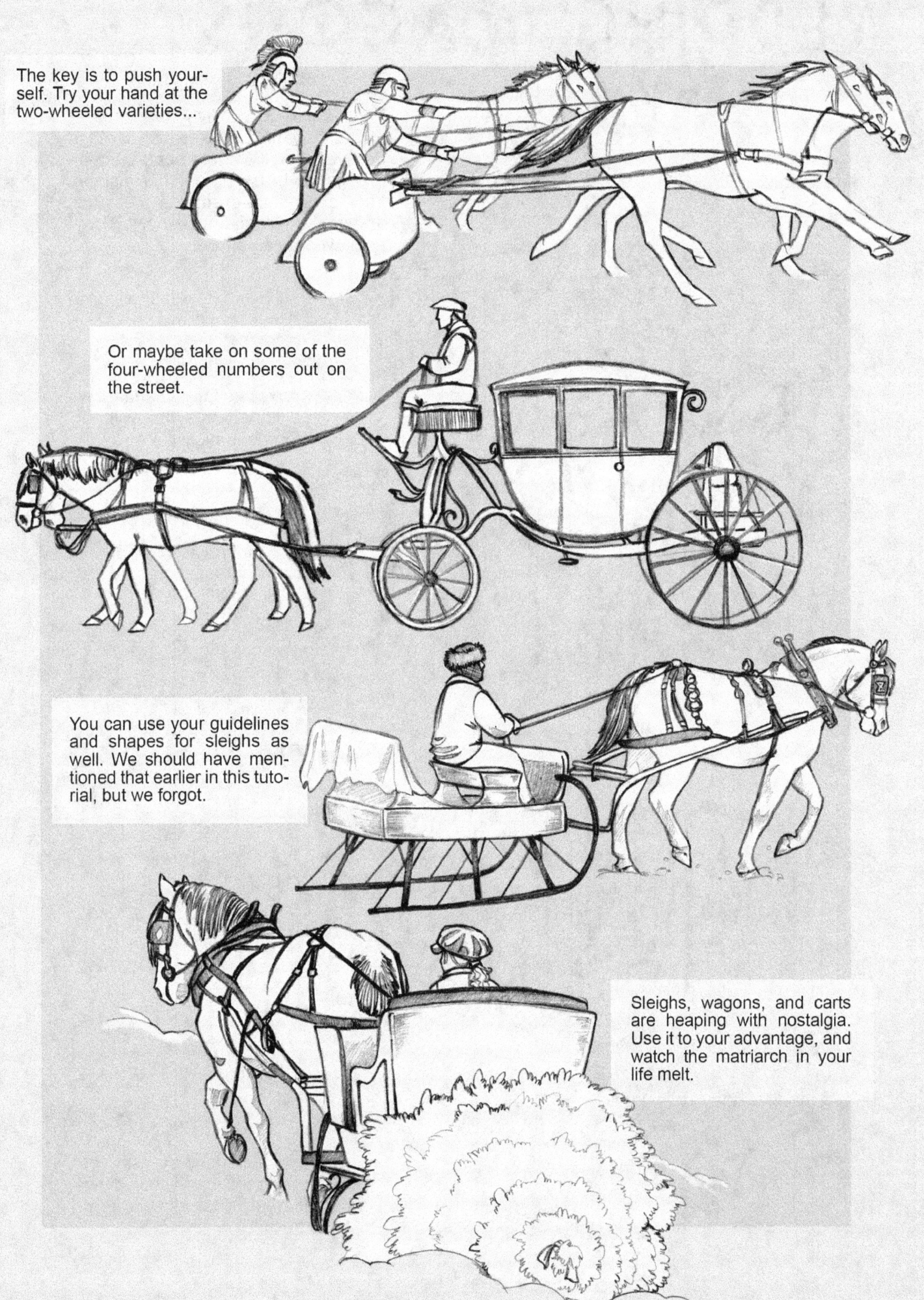

The key is to push yourself. Try your hand at the two-wheeled varieties...

Or maybe take on some of the four-wheeled numbers out on the street.

You can use your guidelines and shapes for sleighs as well. We should have mentioned that earlier in this tutorial, but we forgot.

Sleighs, wagons, and carts are heaping with nostalgia. Use it to your advantage, and watch the matriarch in your life melt.

WEDDING WAGONS

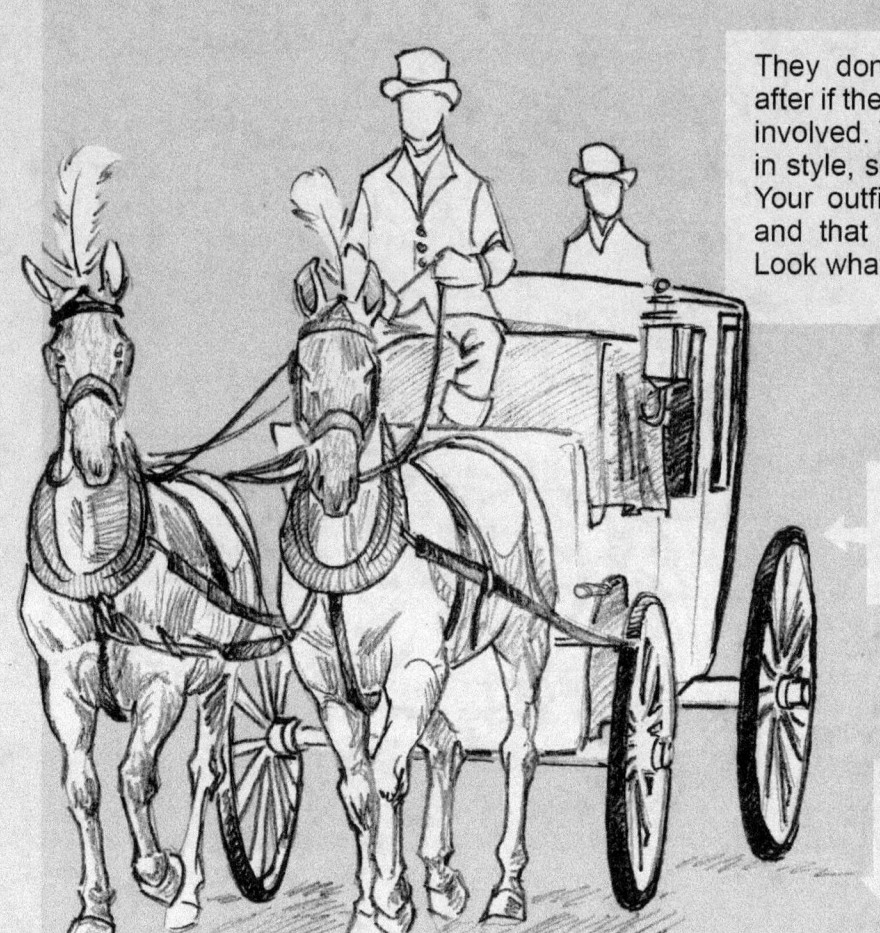

They don't get to live happily ever after if there isn't a horse and carriage involved. You'll want to send them off in style, so brush up on your fashion. Your outfit should send a message, and that message is usually, "Hey! Look what I can afford!"

A classic fairy-tale team with a victorian-style flair will get the job done nicely.

In India, a pair of Marwari-horses may draw the happy couple in an open carriage.

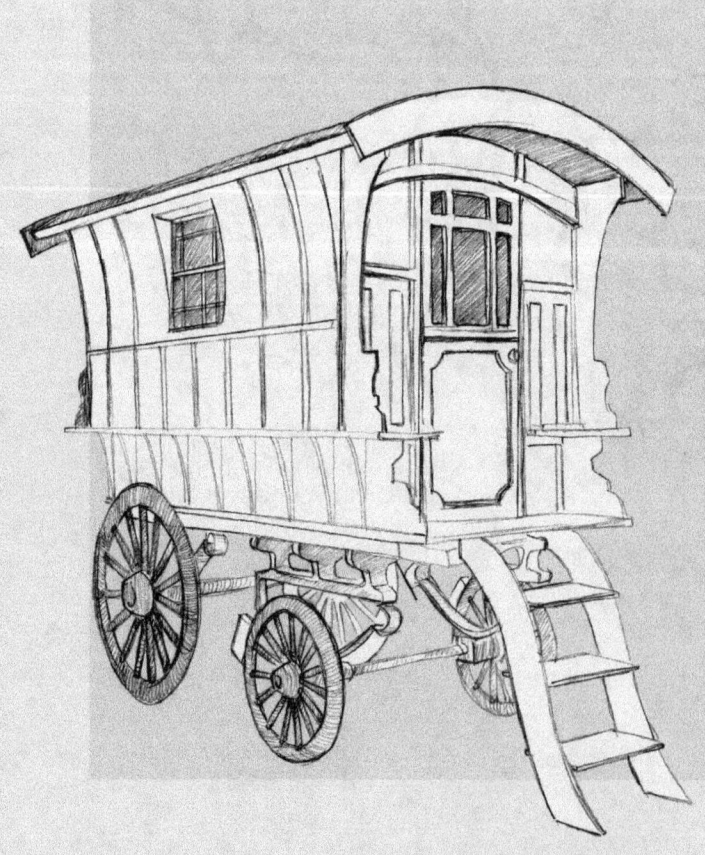

Even gypsies need a set of wheels. Notice: carriages often have different sized wheels from front to back.

SHADING TIPS

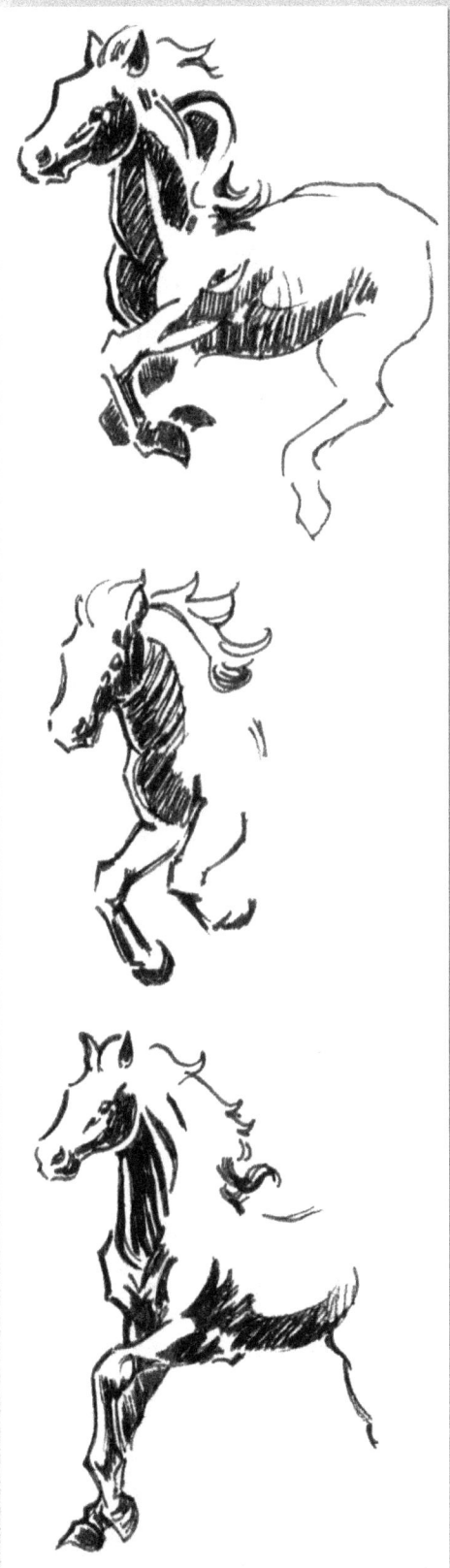

Tips of a shadowy nature is what we'll take a quick gander at. Shading can be a frustrating trick to master but it's necessary, and all you need have to ace it is: 1.) patience 2.) perseverance and 3.) a pencil from another planet. So hang with me for a moment. As a horse moves, different muscle groups are pronounced and shadowed.

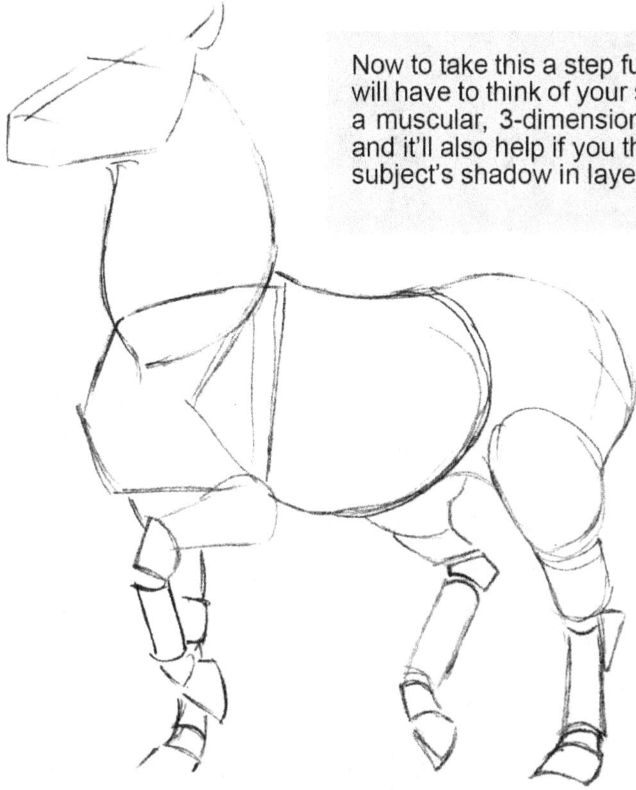

Now to take this a step further, you will have to think of your subject as a muscular, 3-dimensional object, and it'll also help if you think of our subject's shadow in layers.

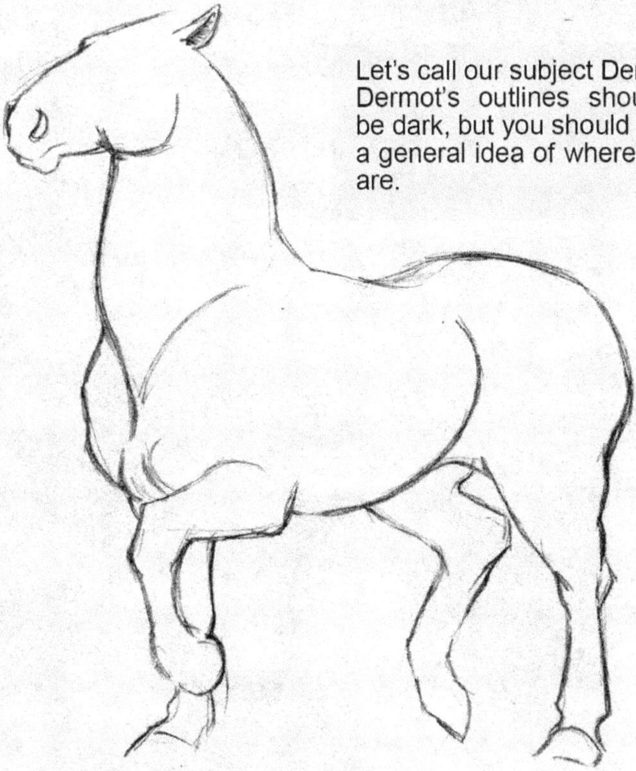

Let's call our subject Dermot. Dermot's outlines shouldn't be dark, but you should have a general idea of where they are.

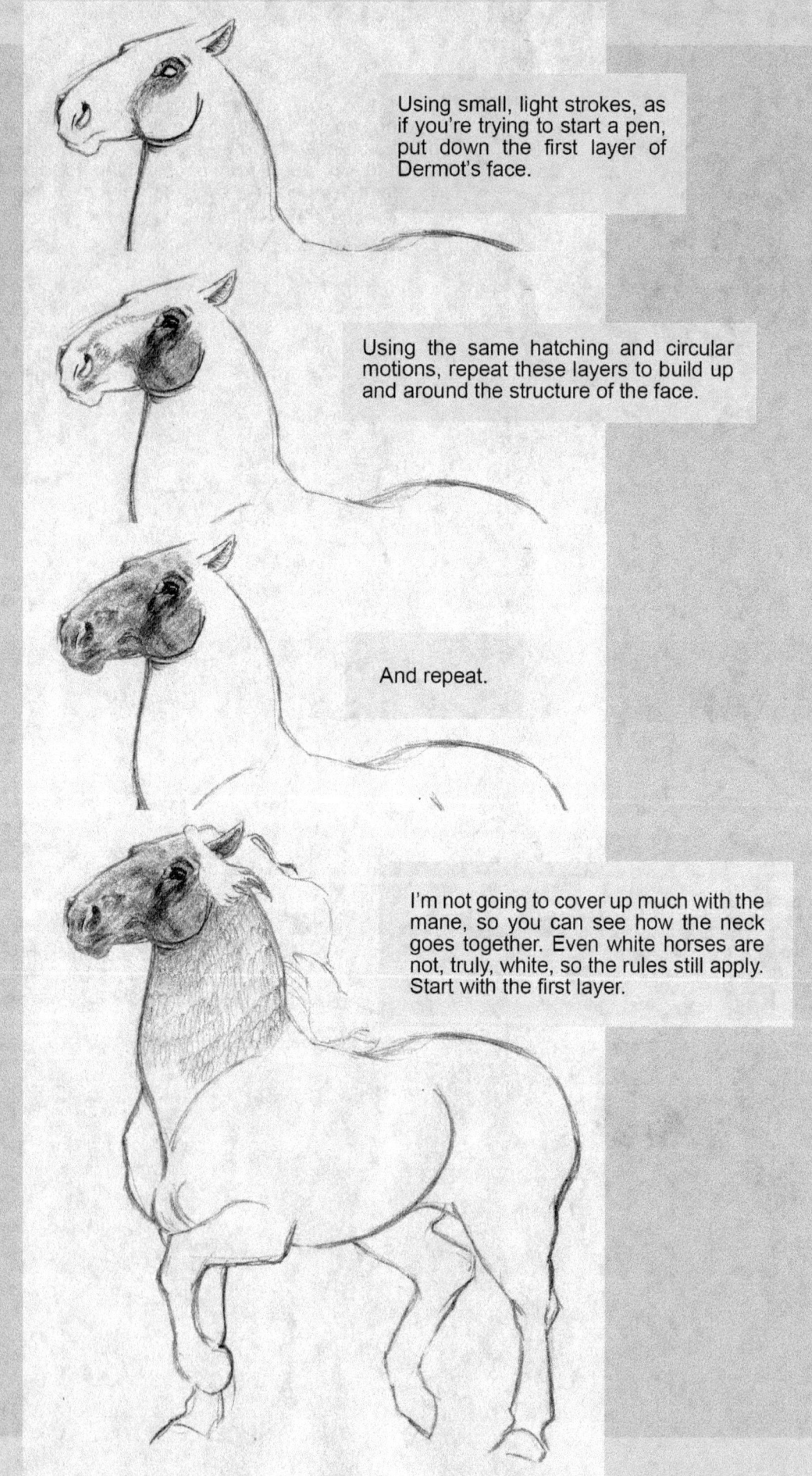

Using small, light strokes, as if you're trying to start a pen, put down the first layer of Dermot's face.

Using the same hatching and circular motions, repeat these layers to build up and around the structure of the face.

And repeat.

I'm not going to cover up much with the mane, so you can see how the neck goes together. Even white horses are not, truly, white, so the rules still apply. Start with the first layer.

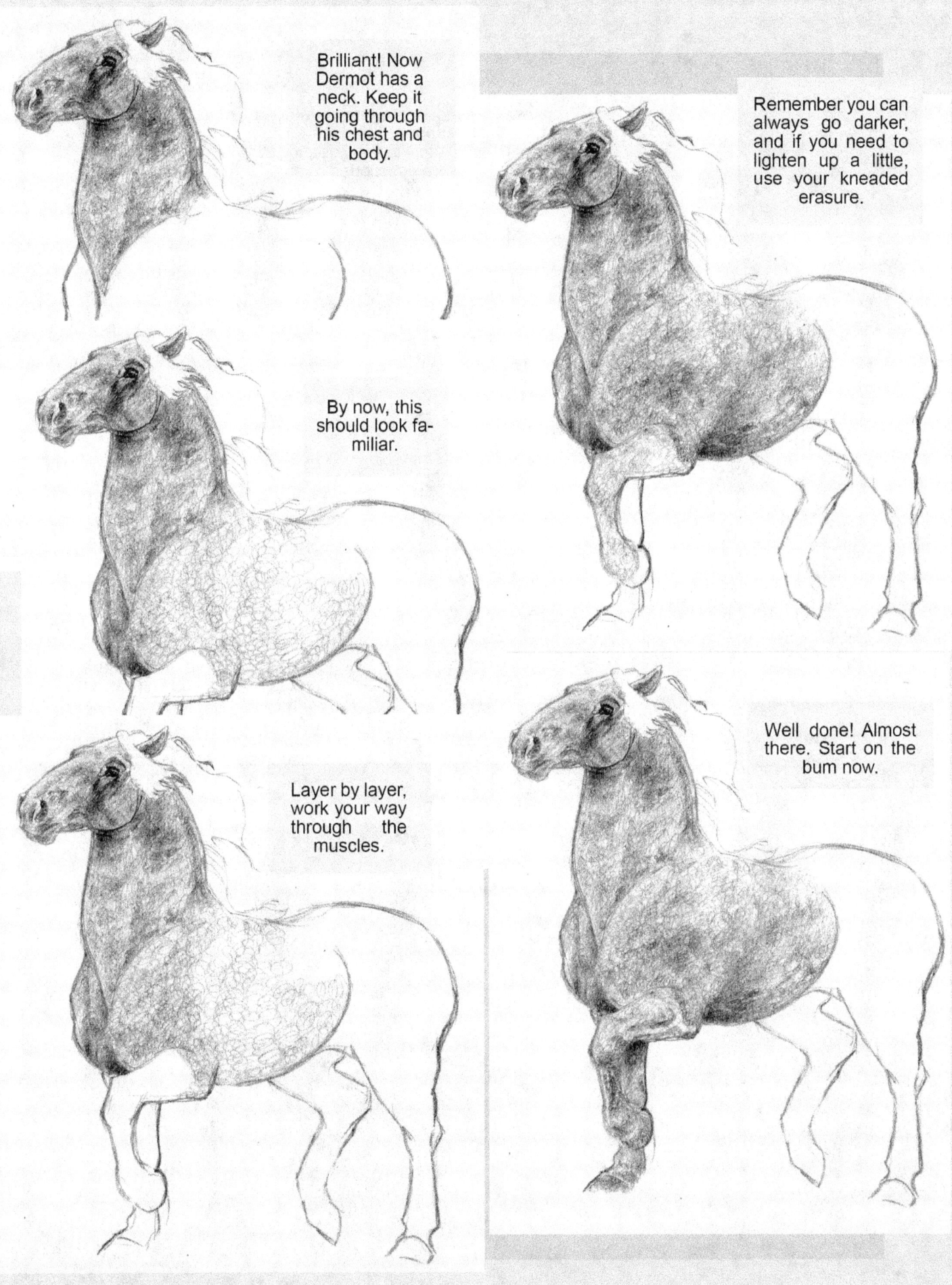

Brilliant! Now Dermot has a neck. Keep it going through his chest and body.

Remember you can always go darker, and if you need to lighten up a little, use your kneaded erasure.

By now, this should look familiar.

Layer by layer, work your way through the muscles.

Well done! Almost there. Start on the bum now.

Use your amazing knowledge to layers to continually overlap and darken your shadows. Think of your weight bearing leg in three sections.

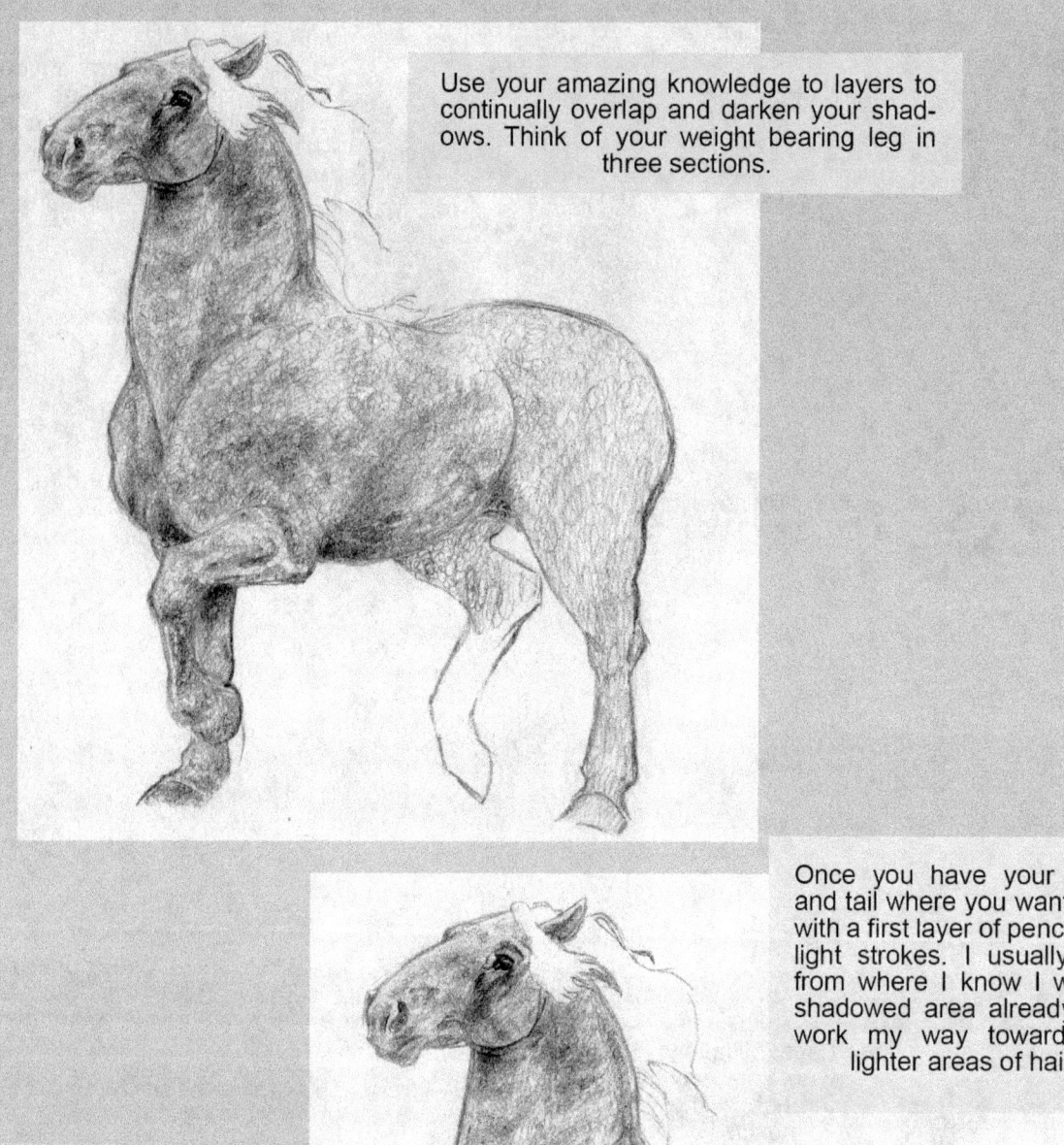

Once you have your mane and tail where you want, start with a first layer of pencil. Use light strokes. I usually start from where I know I want a shadowed area already, and work my way towards the lighter areas of hair.

Dermot deserves a fabulous tail and shadows for the hair follow the same rules of layers as the rest of his body.

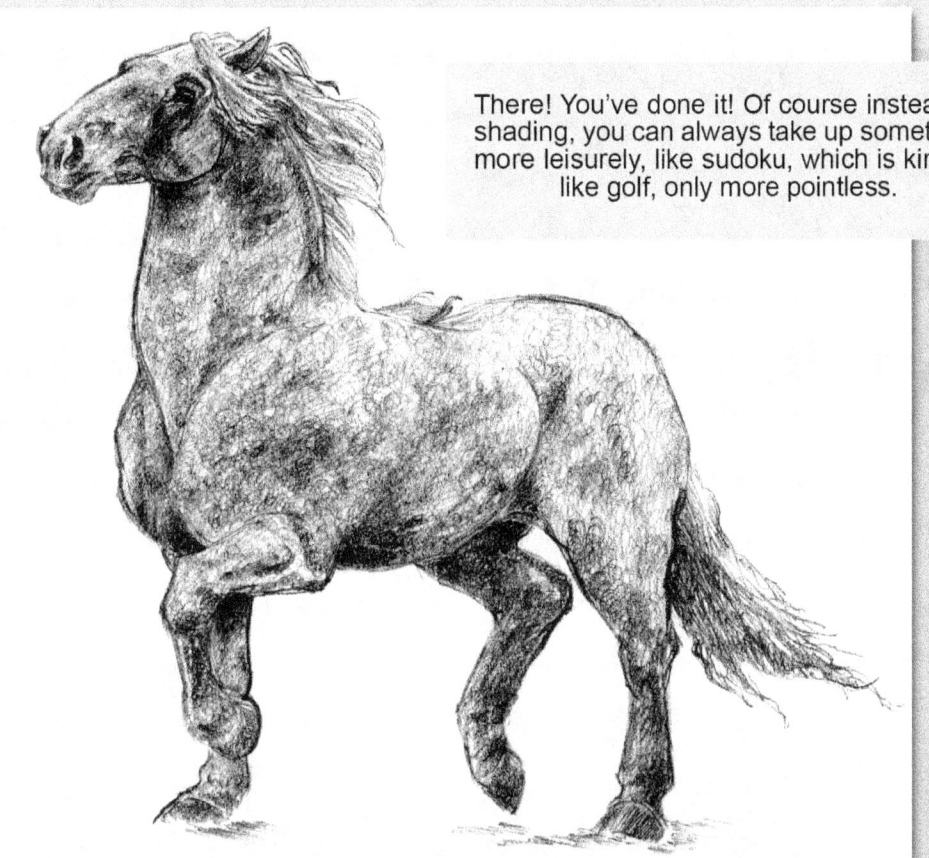

There! You've done it! Of course instead of shading, you can always take up something more leisurely, like sudoku, which is kind of like golf, only more pointless.

Working from headshots will help you better understand the highlights and shadows of a horse's face.

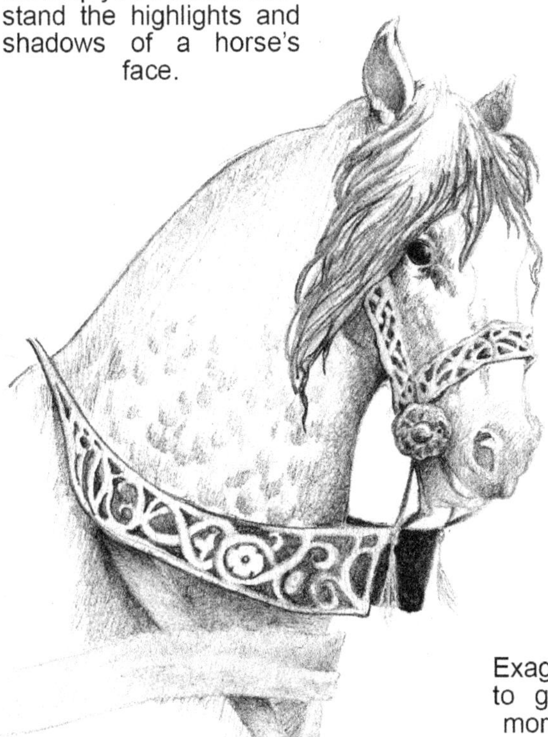

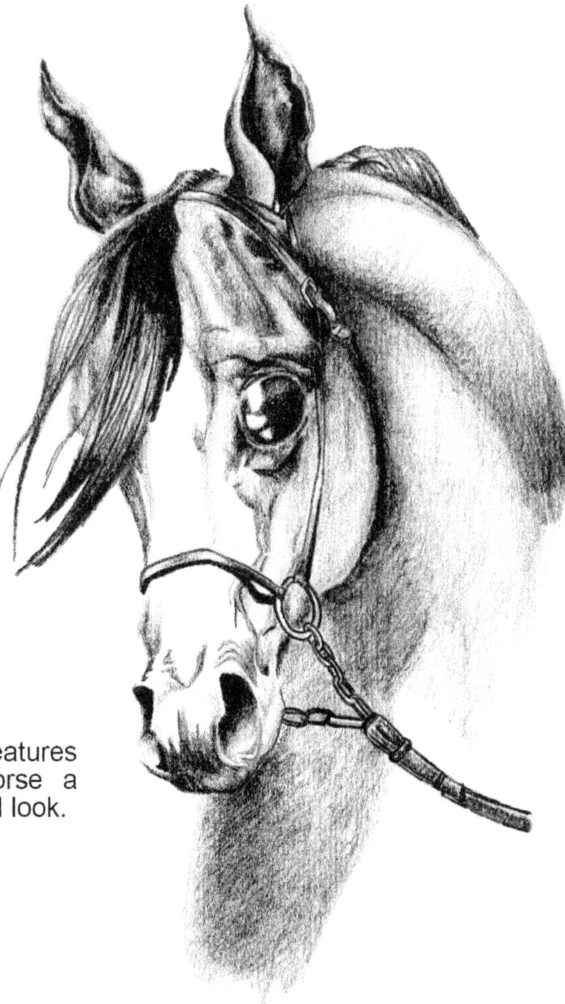

Exaggerate the features to give your horse a more caricatured look.

HAPPY TRAILS

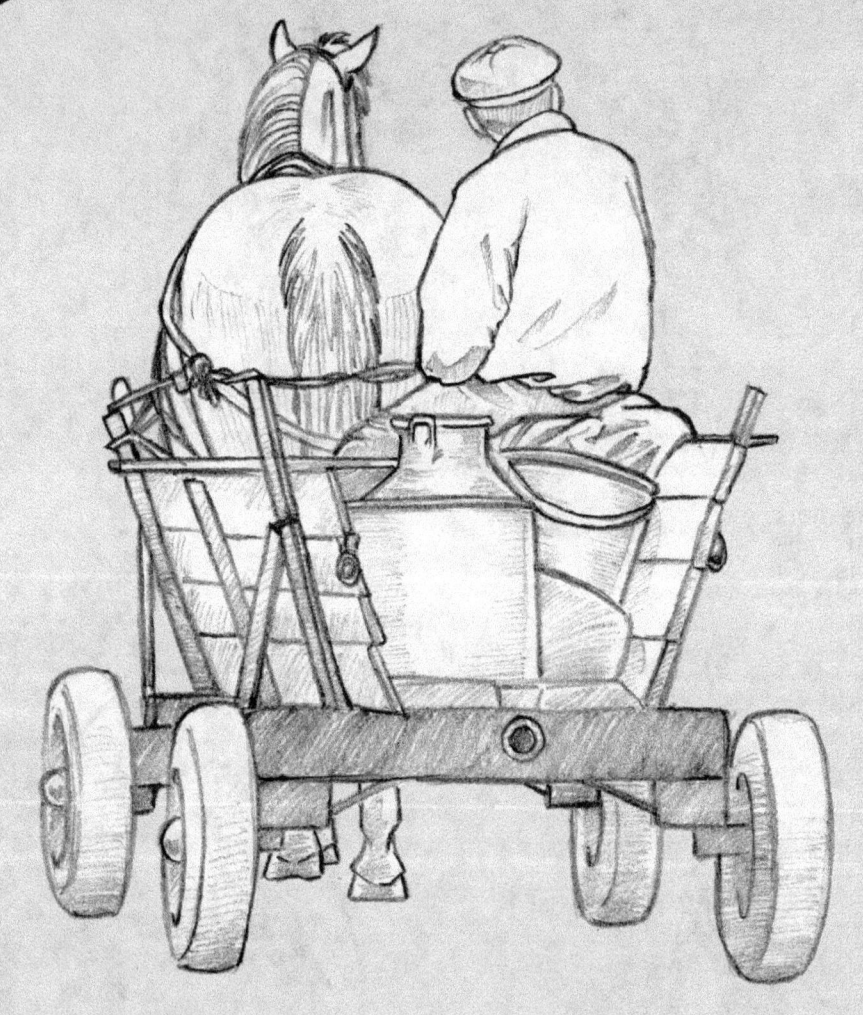

CREDITS

I would like to thank the following people for their creativity, dedication, goodwill, and spunk, without which, this book would have been impossible.

There are people in this world who are just brilliant for letting the rest of us see the world through their eyes and a camera lens. What I'm trying to say in a rather wordy way, is a huge thank you to these inspiring stock photographers:

Anne-Grietje Stock - Germany
http://ponystock.deviantart.com

Emma Louise - United Kingdom
http://zememz.deviantart.com

Darren Fiander - United Kingdom
http://darrenfiander.deviantart.com

Meegan - United States
http://pilgrimsoul.deviantart.com

To all the gracious people who have opened their doors, homes, shops, and booths, to the patrons who turn out for the shows and conventions, and to all those behind the scenes, who keep things happening year after year, I salute you.

And last, but not least, to the fans. Without your voice and support, none of this could have ever happened, and I would be forced to take a real job. I am sincerely grateful.

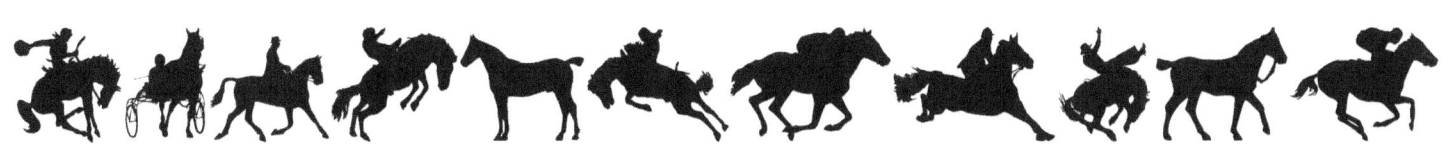